Fundraising
for Churches

12 Keys to Success Every Church Leader Should Know

Linda Wise McNay, PhD
Sarah B. Matthews, CFRE

What people are saying about *Fundraising for Churches: 12 Keys to Success Every Church Leader Should Know...*

From theory to practice, this book will guide congregations on their stewardship journey. Every page has tried-and-true ideas for each step of cultivating generosity and raising resources for the ministry. I will keep it within arm's reach as I teach and lead others in successful fundraising.

Rev. Dr. Bob Winstead
Director of the Academy of Church Business Administration and
Assistant Professor of Practical Theology
Candler School of Theology, Emory University

Fundraising for Churches *is a book chock-full of practical, realistic strategies for church leaders to put into practice. Most pastors and leaders approach the subject with a certain amount of dread and feelings of inadequacy. McNay and Matthews have written a clear and thorough work that should help remove some of that anxiety.*

Jonathan Spencer
Hospice Chaplain, Mesun Health Services, Inc.

McNay and Matthews have produced a comprehensive guide for bringing nonprofit fundraising strategies into the congregational arena. Their book provides year-round and multiyear strategies for successfully funding ministry in the years ahead. Your church will make significant gains in receiving money by taking Linda's and Sarah's recommended actions.

Ruben Swint
Generosity Guy

Fundraising for Churches, by Sarah Matthews and Linda McNay is not simply a "how to" book about church fundraising and stewardship. It is, more importantly, a "why to" book. It's a book dedicated to helping the reader thrive in the area of resource development and to have a good time while doing so. Every minister should keep this book within arm's reach on her/his desk and have copies to distribute to volunteer leaders.

Richard W. Felton
Executive Director, TENS (The Episcopal Network for Stewardship)

As someone who has been a stewardship consultant for over fifteen years and who's worked with dozens of churches, let me say that Matthews and McNay have hit the bull's-eye with both content and presentation of this tough subject matter. This basic fundraising "how to" covers a lot of ground and gives readers a lot to think about, while offering value to all churches regardless of parish size, resources, or objectives. Their wisdom and experience on direct fundraising strategies and techniques borrowed from the nonprofit world are presented clearly and, in my view, are sound practices to consider.

Mal Underwood
Stewardship Consultant, Episcopal Diocese of Atlanta

Fundraising is not taught in seminaries. Yet when clergy take over the reigns of a parish, the congregation's expectation is that they will hit the ground running and create new, inspiring ways to raise money. This easy-to-absorb and practical "how to" should be on the shelf of every clergy and lay fundraiser in the church today.

Cynthia Cannon McWhirter
Executive Director, The Consortium of Endowed Episcopal Parishes

McNay and Matthews address the fears and roadblocks we all face in fundraising; and provide simple, effective steps to lead to fundraising success.

Dr. Sheila Bookout
Senior Pastor, Haygood United Methodist Church

I read the book. I like it a lot. A lot! Because of my schedule, I took it on reluctantly. As it turned out, it was an absolute joy.

Jerry Panas
Author and Executive Partner, Jerold Panas, Linzy & Partners

This easy-to-read book is as much about faith-raising as it is about fundraising. Indeed, they are wonderfully intertwined. In each chapter of this book comes the blessed reminder that all we are and have are God's. That, and how that knowledge can and will transform us and the world. Contained here is real world wisdom about how to partner with God to fund and enlarge God's mission among us. Much needed!

The Rt. Reverend Rob Wright, DD
Bishop, The Episcopal Diocese of Atlanta

Such a great resource . Adaptable ideas and wise counsel by fundraising experts who know and love the church. A guide to stewardship tweaks or a major makeover to benefit your church and its ministry.

Suzii Paynter
Executive Coordinator, Cooperative Baptist Fellowship

McNay and Matthews have done the impossible: they've taken two taboo subjects, religion and money, and put them into an illustrative how-to manual to educate faith communities on the power and grace of stewardship. **Fundraising for Churches** *is a must-read for anyone who seeks tools and communication tactics to talk about money, faith, and stewardship.*

Nancy Zintak
Regional Vice President — Atlanta, Caron Treatment Centers / Caron Solutions

Fundraising for Churches *brilliantly illustrates the principles and techniques for building a robust fundraising operation. I found the book to be very relevant to the challenges many of us are facing, especially given the ever-changing philanthropic landscape. McNay and Matthews have done a beautiful job of providing recommendations to achieve financial sustainability within the context of a faith-based environment.*

Paul Deckard
Finance Trustee, Unitarian Universalist Congregation of Atlanta

Think of this book as everything you ever needed to know about church fundraising—but had no idea what to even ask! Churches of all sizes are struggling today with their finances, and clergy and staff must get more savvy about how to raise funds in biblical, graceful, and effective ways. Fortunately for us, McNay and Matthews are uniquely qualified to provide, in an accessible and compelling way, the information and expertise churches desperately need so they can fulfill their mission in this needful world.

The Rev. Peter M. Wallace
Episcopal priest, Day1 radio program producer and host *(Day1.org),* **and author of** *The Passionate Jesus*

Fundraising for Churches:
12 Keys to Success Every Church Leader Should Know

One of the **In the Trenches**™ series

Published by

CharityChannel Press, an imprint of CharityChannel LLC

424 Church Street, Suite 2000

Nashville, TN 37219 USA

CharityChannel.com

ISBN Print Book: 978-1-938077-83-8

Library of Congress Control Number: 2017934194

13 12 11 10 9 8 7 6 5 4 3 2 1

Printed in the United States of America

This and most CharityChannel Press books are available at special quantity discounts for bulk purchases for sales promotions, premiums, fundraising, or educational use. For information, contact CharityChannel Press, 424 Church Street, Suite 2000, Nashville, TN 37219 USA. +1 949-589-5938

Publisher's Acknowledgments

This book was produced by a team dedicated to excellence; please send your feedback to editors@ charitychannel.com.

We first wish to acknowledge the tens of thousands of peers who call charitychannel.com their online professional home. Your enthusiastic support for the **In the Trenches**™ series is the wind in our sails.

Members of the team who produced this book include:

Editors

Acquisitions Editor: Linda Lysakowski

Manuscript Editor: Stephen Nill

Production

In the Trenches Series Design: Deborah Perdue

Layout Editor: Stephen C. Nill

Administrative

CharityChannel LLC: Stephen Nill, CEO

Marketing and Public Relations: John Millen and Linda Lysakowski

About the Authors

Linda Wise McNay, PhD

Linda Wise McNay is an independent fundraising consultant with Our Fundraising Search in Atlanta. She has just completed her tenth year of consulting and has served more than one hundred clients. Linda's nonprofit background includes work with both higher and secondary education, the arts, and human service organizations and has included work in capital campaigns, annual fund, planned giving, membership, strategic planning, and development search.

In addition to assisting many faith-based clients in their fundraising efforts, Linda has helped her own Baptist and Methodist churches with their stewardship.

Prior to years of consulting work with Alexander Haas, Linda served as chief development officer for the High Museum of Art, leading its efforts to raise $95 million to bring great art from the Louvre and China to the Atlanta community. During her tenure, she also managed the execution of an endowment campaign, initiated the institution's first full-time planned giving effort, and increased the museum's membership to a record fifty thousand. During this time, Linda served as national president of the Art Museum Development Association. She currently serves on the Directors Counsel, University of Kentucky Art Museum.

Linda served as director of advancement at Pace Academy, a K-12 private school in Atlanta. At Pace, she led the school's largest and most successful capital fundraising campaign with a goal of $15 million. The campaign was an overwhelming success, reaching goal ahead of schedule, under budget and with 95 percent parent participation and 100 percent board and 100 percent faculty/staff participation.

In higher education, Linda has held positions including vice president of the Georgia Foundation for Independent Colleges; executive director of the Emory Challenge Fund at Emory University; director of development at the Georgia Institute of Technology, and alumni and development roles at her alma mater, Transylvania University. In her career, Linda has been responsible for raising more than $250 million for her employers and clients.

She is the author of *Fundraising for Schools: 8 Keys to Success Every Head of School Should Know* and *Fundraising for Museums: 8 Keys to Success Every Museum Leader Should Know* as well as the author of numerous articles for publication. Linda is a regular speaker and presenter at workshops and conferences.

Linda earned her doctorate in the philosophy of higher education from Georgia State University. Her doctoral dissertation was entitled, *The Relative Cost Effectiveness of Three Direct Mail Techniques on Non-Alumni Prospects.* She also earned a master of business administration degree, specializing in personnel administration, from the University of Kentucky; and a bachelor of arts degree from Transylvania University in Lexington, Kentucky.

Linda and her architect husband, Gary, have two adult sons.

Sarah B. Matthews, CFRE

Sarah B. Matthews has served as a financial resources consultant for more than eleven years. She currently serves Visiting Nurse Health System as the director of individual giving. Actively involved in church ministry since 1989, she has worked with churches in most mainline denominations from Rhode Island to Florida, but because Sarah is an Episcopal Church rector's wife, she is keenly aware of the challenges involved in funding campaigns in churches.

Her consulting work has been with Cargill Associates (Texas) and the Episcopal Church Foundation (New York) and independently through Matthews Consulting (Georgia), and has helped her clients raise over $10 million. Her breadth of knowledge and experience include discernment and visioning services, feasibility studies, capital campaigns, annual fund drives, asset mapping and strategic planning, and leadership development. She is also a speaker and trainer at the diocesan and conference levels and has been the director of development at a small Christian university.

Sarah is currently serving on the advisory board for Emmaus House, a ministry of the Diocese of Atlanta, and served on the Commission on Stewardship for the Diocese of Atlanta for eight years. Sarah is a member of the Association of Fundraising Professionals and has earned the Certified Fund Raising Executive designation. Sarah is a past board member, having served as secretary/treasurer for The Episcopal Network for Stewardship (2011-2014).

Before focusing on church consulting, Sarah served as the founding director of the Kingsport Community Foundation. She directed the education and training efforts of a large national Christian association, and spent eight years in the hospitality and meeting planning industry.

Sarah earned a BS in communications from the University of Tennessee, Knoxville.

Dedication

Linda Wise McNay

This book is dedicated to Dr. Sheila Bookout, pastor of Haygood United Methodist Church. She is great at fundraising even while handling her myriad of tasks as senior minister, engaging as a mother and daughter, and battling some serious health issues. Sheila, you are my hero!

Sarah B. Matthews

This book is dedicated to my husband, The Rev. Dan Matthews, Jr. I am thankful for his loving support of all my endeavors, especially the encouragement to develop professionally by earning my CFRE certification and by writing this book. I have learned so much in the last three decades from Dan about stewardship and spirituality as well as writing and public speaking. He has always been my greatest cheerleader and my best teacher.

Authors' Acknowledgments

Linda's Acknowledgments

After consulting with more than one hundred clients, perhaps it is my faith-based clients that have touched me the most. I have worked with Christian schools and camps and church-affiliated organizations and it is really something special when our meetings begin or end in prayer. How can we not be successful when there is a higher power involved?

I am thankful for my family and friends for cheering me on in this, my third book. It is written for churches who need to start raising money like other nonprofits—before they fall behind in this competitive fundraising environment. It has been a pleasure to work with writing partner Sarah Matthews, and I appreciate Stephen and Linda and all the folks at CharityChannel Press for their continuing faith in me.

Bless their hearts!

Sarah's Acknowledgements

Stewardship has long been at the foundation of my beliefs. This notion that all we are and that all we have belongs to God, and how we choose to use (or misuse) these gifts from God is at the heart of what it means for me to live as a Christian. In my early years, it was just a concept that I applied to our financial giving. Then, through the teachings and conversations of others, it has grown to a much broader understanding for me.

I am grateful to all the teachers I have encountered—whether through their life as an example or through their writings and workshops—as well as the lessons I learned when consulting with churches. The stories I heard, and the testimonies revealed to me, have humbled me each time. This work of raising money to fund mission and ministry for churches is truly God's work.

I especially appreciate the support and guidance of my writing partner—Linda, you are a great writing mentor and friend! Thanks, also, to Stephen and everyone at CharityChannel Press for believing in an untested writer like me!

Contents

Summary of Chapters

Foreword

If your church would benefit from additional funds (and what church wouldn't), you have precisely the right book in your hands—*Fundraising for Churches*. Every clergy, every church leader, every member of a church board should have a copy.

To my way of thinking, the book is the very best in its field. The subtitle is: "12 Keys to Success Every Church Leader Should Know." It's all there. There's everything you would want to know about annual operating support, capital campaigns, and endowment for building and maintenance.

It's wonderfully written. I found myself finishing it in one sitting. Then rereading it, underlining, and writing in the margins.

The authors, Sarah Matthews and Linda Wise McNay, tell us in an early paragraph, "You will have a clear understanding of how to raise meaningful dollars, and you will have the confidence to launch a highly ambitious and successful fundraising campaign." They deliver on that promise.

Here's what I particularly like about the book. You will, also. I'm reminded that it's not really about money. It's about the human spirit. Dreams. And high aspirations.

I'm positive that if you emphasize the spiritual life of the church, the money will follow.

When I first saw the title, I wasn't enthralled. Well, that's the truth of it. I thought it ought to have more zip, more *snap, crackle, and pop.*

But actually, the title says something about the book. It's basic, fundamental, pure fundraising. There's not a lot of philosophy. Just the essential nuts and bolts of raising funds. From A to Z.

For instance, they answer the question about how much a parishioner should contribute to a church. And whether clergy should know what members of the congregation give. I've wrestled with those questions myself.

You will also read about why one church returned a valuable Picasso. I kept thinking as I read the passage, "Don't return the painting. Find a way to keep it."

I have found that people do not want to just give money away, they want to give to programs and causes that touch lives in magical ways. The authors make it quite clear that people will give generously and sacrificially when the need is clearly and passionately demonstrated.

We are reminded that God is the giver, the true donor. The job of the Christian is not to begrudgingly discern how much should be given away, but to make certain of the reality that God is the donor. I love a little poem I have saved and used over the years:

Angel, must I give again, I ask in dismay,

And must I keep giving and giving and giving it away?

Oh no, said the Angel, his glance pierced me through,

Just keep giving till the Lord stops giving to you.

The book presents a very strong case for tithing. There are seven scripture references that have a stewardship-theme. I went back to my Bible and read each one. This was powerful. Interestingly, there are sixty-seven references to tithing in the Bible.

There is an outline for what should be included in all the details of a campaign. It is priceless. Along with it, a chart of the suggested hierarchy of the campaign. There's even a lesson on who should chair the program.

I had one small quarrel. But it's really a minor issue. There's reference in the book that people give to people. That's a hoary verity in our profession—that people give to people. It's been repeated *ad nauseam*.

Actually, people don't give to people. I believe what is meant is that people give more when they are asked in person. People don't give to people—they give to exciting, important, spiritual causes.

The book also deals with the importance of one-on-one personal solicitations. We know you don't get milk from a cow by sending a letter. And you don't get milk from a cow by calling on a phone. You get milk by sitting next to the cow and milking it.

There is a superb section on how to get the appointment. My experience is if you get the appointment, you're 85 percent on your way to getting the gift. The authors tell us how to ask for the gift, what you do when you arrive for the meeting, and what should be said to get the gift.

And they tell you how you respond to, "I'll need to think about it." Or what do you do if there are objections. The book answers all of this. I can tell you that when you finish this section, you are indeed ready to ask.

The chapter on capital campaigns is as good as I've ever read. It takes you from the planning to the feasibility study, to the case statement, to the ask. Follow this and you are assured of success.

There's some good news I want to share with you. The authors report that it's clear that a capital campaign does not affect annual giving; that, quite the contrary, it helps increase it. That's been my experience, also.

Every church leader, in fact every member of the church, should read the section on endowment. That's the future of your church. Planned giving and bequests should be stressed throughout the year with congregants.

You read that people who make large gifts generally do not make quick decisions. They'll need a little cultivation. I remind you that you don't make a pickle by sprinkling a little vinegar over a cucumber! You have to immerse it.

The larger the gift, the more likely it is to be emotional. Large gifts are visceral, not cerebral.

I've faced the question of what do you do with members who have not turned in their pledge card. This can be awkward. This book has the answer.

There's a wonderful schedule for how to prepare for a fall pledge drive. I've looked it over. It is fail-proof. If you follow that, you simply can't miss.

To my way of thinking, one of the very best sections is on stewardship. The ultimate goal for the church is to develop disciples and to support them as they grow. This takes time.

I could go on and on. The book is wonderfully easy to read and packed to the brim and overflowing with powerful and helpful information.

This book doesn't belong in the church library. It belongs on every pastor's desk. And in the hands of every church leader.

Fundraising for Churches is one of those rare books that takes you by the hand and truly leads you to successful fundraising.

Jerold Panas
Author, Speaker
Executive Partner, Jerold Panas, Linzy & Partners

Introduction

Just like any other nonprofit organization, your church or faith-based organization needs to raise money. This includes annual operating support as well as capital and endowment for building and maintenance.

As we mention in **Chapter One,** of the $373 billion that was given away in the United States in 2015, one-third, or nearly $120 billion, went to religious causes. While this is clearly a huge sum, that percentage has been declining for years, from over half of the money given away.

No one knows exactly why. It could be that we as a nation are less faithful than our ancestors. Clearly, we are more philanthropic every year. Perhaps there are just more choices for giving. No matter the cause, what can be done about this decline in giving to churches?

We believe that churches and other faith-based organizations need to become more adept at raising funds, just like any other type of nonprofit. No longer can we be idle bystanders. We can't wait to see what comes in the collection plate. We cannot depend on people to embrace tithing. We cannot wait for the Lord to provide. There are things we can do to help the process along.

Our book is written with church leaders in mind—whether they be clergy or other staff members, or lay leaders and volunteers. By the time you have finished reading *Fundraising for Churches: 12 Keys to Success Every Church Leader Should Know,* you will have a clear understanding of how to raise meaningful dollars, and you will have the confidence to launch a highly ambitious and successful fundraising campaign.

In **Chapter One** you will find that fundraising is everyone's job: the pastor's, the lay leadership's, the staff's, and other volunteers'. The secrets to success in any fundraising campaign include crafting a compelling case for support; enlisting strong, committed leadership; and drafting and executing a written strategy/plan of action.

Why should a parishioner contribute to your church? What differentiates your church from your members' college or school or another nonprofit? You should have an elevator speech that you can give at any time to friends or strangers. Your lay leaders and staff members need to have those same talking points. This case for support forms the basis for all your funding efforts from letters or emails to specific proposals. You must all be on the same page. What would a gift to your church enable it to do that it is not now doing? What will your church not be able to do without the gift?

Of the three secrets to success, leadership may be the most critical. You can have a mediocre case for support, but if you have a charismatic leader you can still raise money. This fundraising leadership can come from the pastor, the lay leadership, volunteer committee, or other staff members. This should be a team effort. Having 100 percent support from your team is critical to raising funds from others not as close to the mission of your church. Your designated fundraising team must be willing and able to not just give money, but to ask others to join them as well.

You must have a written fundraising plan. This can be implemented by you, by your fundraising team, by volunteers or staff, or by a combination of people. The plan must include multiple ways of giving and be offered to all your constituents. It must include appropriate follow-up to position your church for future fundraising activities.

How you develop and prepare the materials for your parishioners to review and to reflect upon during the annual pledge drive can make or break your efforts. A mission-driven budget articulates, in narrative format with graphics, photographs, and text (not just numbers) the many ministries of the church that are enabled by the gifts of parishioners.

Chapter Two outlines the steps to creating a budget that reflects how the money is being spent in a compelling and transparent way, yet doesn't bore your members with spreadsheets. A budget created this way reminds people of the good work that is happening in their church while reporting on the impact of their ministry and money.

Leadership as shown in **Chapter Three** shows how an annual pledge drive can take several forms. We know from experience that people will give when the need is demonstrated. As the leader of the church, you know better than anyone the stories that demonstrate that need: how people's lives have been changed by the programs of your church. Plan to passionately communicate the need in creative and compelling ways.

The pastor can also set the tone for this campaign among staff. You can help the stewardship team by identifying and recruiting people who are spiritually grounded enough to take on this important ministry. Don't leave this job of funding the church ministries to those who volunteer; your team members should be recruited for their specific skill set. This chapter will include what to look for in your congregation, as well as job descriptions that include the anticipated time commitment for each job.

As a spiritual leader of the annual pledge drive, you must be the first to prayerfully examine your giving habits and respond in a sacrificial and transparent way. In turn, those serving on the stewardship ministry team must also be committed to approaching their giving to the church in a spiritual and prayerful manner.

We will also cover the pros and cons of having the pastor serve as a solicitor in fundraising for the church, as well as tackle the tough question: Should the pastor know what the people are giving?

Timelines, themes, and a drill sergeant will be necessary to keep your plan from going into the ditch. Your written strategy (**Chapter Four**) to get you through the annual pledge drive will be the document that keeps you on track from this planning stage to the final follow-up call. Working with our sample timelines, you will learn how to sketch out each activity and assign it to the right people to do the work. Regular meetings should be scheduled at the beginning of this cycle, and if you target October for the weeks of your main drive, then beginning your planning in March is not too early.

There are many themes and approaches you can take. Remember that there are several reasons you have these four weeks of intense focus on funding the ministries. One is to showcase how the ministries that your members funded last year have changed people's lives. Written messages from the refugee family you helped, photos from the youth mission trip, and testimonials in church during announcements are all effective ways of demonstrating your impact. Another reason to take several weeks to complete your annual campaign is to get the pledge cards in the hands of the members, and to give contributors a way to return them. While the delivery method may vary from year to year—and it should—the main components of your campaign do not.

The chair of your stewardship committee must be the drill sergeant: the one who is most focused on getting the team across the finish line. Much of the work can and should be done in the spring and over the summer, so that when the fall comes around implementation of the components is all that is left.

Who are your prospects for giving to your church? The clergy, the staff, lay leaders, members, visitors, seniors, adults, young people, even children; and each category deserves its own strategy. In **Chapter Five** we show you how prospects capable of giving larger amounts should be identified and cultivated and solicited personally for maximum results. Others can be solicited and involved through email, mail, phone, events, or group meetings.

There are some foundations and organizations that give to faith-based organizations. Include them in your fundraising plan as well as others in your community who have benefited from the good works of your congregation.

You are a member of a community of faith, and it is expected that God and the Bible will be a part of this conversation. Contrary to some notions, using scripture as a basis for fundraising in a church is not manipulative; it is used for several basic reasons. First, it models how we should approach our individual relationship to money. In the New Testament, Jesus told many stories about people and their relationship to money. In fact, except for the Kingdom of God, Jesus talked about money more than any other subject. These examples were included in scripture for us to learn about ourselves through them. Use them during your pledge drive so that people can see that the Bible really does speak to us today.

Another advantage churches have is that there is a captive audience, **Chapter Six**. Literally. Each Sunday, your members are gathered for worship and Sunday school. Use that time wisely throughout the year. We would also suggest that since the average member considers regular attendance to be twice a month, that you repeat your message (in different ways) for several weeks.

Annual fund gifts are the lifeblood of any church, **Chapter Seven**. Typically, unrestricted, annual funds are used where the need is greatest. Annual funds do not finance new buildings. Annual funds do not create endowments. Annual funds do not usually provide enough resources to grow an institution. Let's face it; it is just not as sexy to raise money to pay the light bill as it is to build a building.

Of all campaigns, annual campaigns are the least cost effective, especially if you are in the start-up phase. Well-established annual funds with a loyal donor base are less expensive. With new initiatives, the cost to educate and acquire a new donor may equal the amount of money raised in year one. The cost of raising a donor dollar is substantially less than raising a nondonor dollar. Once a donor makes a first gift, that same donor is more likely to return as a donor.

Each year the stewardship team must motivate last year's annual donors to give again, and give at a higher average gift. They must also try to attract new gifts and reattract lapsed donors.

Major gifts can be annual, capital, or endowment in nature and are covered in **Chapter Eight.** The general rule is that the gifts are larger than normal and they may not occur every year. Major gifts typically come from annual donors who have been motivated to give an additional amount for a special project or need. These gifts should be solicited in person and for a specific amount. Solicitors should make sure the prospect knows why their gift is so important now in the life of the church and what will happen as a result of their gift. It is also important to note what will not happen if the gift is not made.

Some donors are motivated by recognition. Named-gift opportunities should be provided. Donor clubs may be established at certain levels. Every attempt should be made to allow donors to make gifts in the most convenient method to them. Memorials or honor gifts can also be a compelling reason for a donor to make a significant contribution.

Most religious institutions are either in a capital campaign, getting ready for a campaign, or finishing a campaign. In **Chapter Nine** on capital campaigns, we review precampaign planning, getting organized, and the role of the clergy and lay leadership, followed by the details of an active campaign and the importance of stewardship.

Capital campaign activities usually stretch out over a five-year period. The first year or two include precampaign planning activities: Does your church have an updated strategic plan? Is there a business plan that follows the strategy? Have you educated and cultivated your congregation? Have your plans been costed out with an architect and/or engineer? Have you conducted an internal and external readiness assessment? Have you evaluated your case for support and do you have a written campaign plan?

The active campaign begins a year or two later with a governing board leadership solicitation, followed by solicitation of your top donors and prospects. Always solicit the best prospects first, followed by the next best prospects. A public phase for the general congregation comes at the end of the campaign when most of the money has been raised.

Years three to five are for stewarding donors. You must do what you promised you would do when you presented them with your case for support. Collect the pledges, manage the funds, and communicate campaign results.

Endowment is critical to the future of religious organizations. How large an endowment should your church have? **Chapter Ten** focuses on how to create and build an endowment for your organization through planned giving and education of your congregation.

Sufficient endowment is critical to the future of faith-based organizations. What is the size of your church's endowment? Some say the optimum size for a church endowment is three to five times your annual budget. You can do the math.

What is the market value of your endowment? How many endowment funds do you have, if any? What is the amount of income from your endowment funds generated for your annual operating budget? These financial questions are important to the future planning of churches.

You know you are ready for endowment building when you have defined your mission, and you have a solid financial base, a growing donor pool, and the highest-quality product for donors to invest in. As with any other type of campaign, the church leadership needs to be committed to endowment for fundraising to be successful. It helps to have a long-term history of annual giving to allow you to profile and prospect among annual donors. And there always needs to be a balance between asking for operating, endowment, and capital needs.

Your members experience over three thousand messages a day telling them how to spend their time and their money. How often and in what ways do you communicate what your church has to offer your members? Once your initial commitment program strategy is laid out, consider what else you should add to the plan to capture the attention of your members and to keep it relevant.

Chapter Eleven features a review of innovations and technology in fundraising for churches. More and more, the people in your congregation are online. Do you communicate digitally with them? What this means for your annual fund drive is several things. Elements of your commitment program can be produced to experience online. You can record some of the live messages given during the church service or Sunday school time and make them available through your website. Have your pledge card downloadable. Or better yet, communicate to your members how they can pay their pledge online. It is especially important to consider how younger generations give. Because they don't write checks—most don't even have any—you should have a way for them to give electronically. Giving kiosks, Square Reader, and online giving will continue to grow due to the habits of this group.

Do your materials reflect the native language of your members? You might consider translating your materials into Spanish if that is the language for a significant number of your members. Many churches these days are including their children and youth in the giving life of the congregation. Marketers are keenly aware that this young generation has more disposable income than any before it. Are you teaching your young people about giving back to others less fortunate?

You have probably heard the complaint, "All we hear about in church is money." While that is not likely the case, it is a common perception. That is where the culture of your church needs to shift from a model that only talks about money and fundraising in the fall, to a community that talks about being stewards of God's gifts to them all year long.

To do this, you must first give the word "stewardship" a rebranding. For decades, we in the church have tarnished its meaning. **Chapter Twelve** will define what it means to be a steward of God's gifts, and give you suggestions on how to talk about being a good steward of these gifts in every season. We will look at the fallacies of the time, talent, and treasure trio, and offer best practices on engaging your congregation in meaningful ways throughout the year. Stewardship will no longer be a dirty word, and attendance during your fall pledge drive won't be low anymore.

Chapter One

Three Secrets to Successful Fundraising

IN THIS CHAPTER

- ---→ How much time should be devoted to fundraising in your church?

- ---→ What are the secrets to successful fundraising for churches?

- ---→ All solicitation methods are not created equally

- ---→ It is not just about asking

In this chapter, you will find that fundraising is everyone's job: the church pastor, the lay leaders, the staff, and other volunteers.

And the secrets to success in any fundraising campaign include crafting a compelling case for support, enlisting strong, committed leadership, and drafting a written strategy/plan of action. These three topics will be covered in greater detail in the next chapters.

Why should a donor contribute to your church? What differentiates your church from another faith-based organization? You should have an elevator speech that you can give at any time to friends or strangers. Your lay leaders and other church members need to have those same talking points. This case for support forms the basis of all your funding efforts, from letters to foundation proposals. And you must all be on the same page. What would a gift enable your church to do that it is not now doing? What will your church *not* be able to do without the gift?

Of those three secrets to fundraising success, leadership may be the most critical. You can have a mediocre case for support, but if you have a charismatic leader, you can still raise money. This fundraising leadership can come from the pastor or other clergy, the lay chair, the development committee, and/ or the development office, if there is one. This should be a team effort. Having 100 percent support from your leadership team is critical to raising funds from others not as close to the church. Your team must be willing and able to not just give money, but to ask others to join them as well.

You must have a written fundraising plan. This can be implemented by you, by your development team, by volunteers, or a combination of people. The plan must include multiple ways of giving and be offered to all your church constituents. It must include appropriate stewardship to position your institution for future fundraising campaigns.

Your church fundraising goals must be clearly defined in your annual plan. These must be reasonable and reachable, communicated with your constituents, and embraced by your church leadership. This is not a burden only for you, but is shared by the church leadership and whatever development team you may have.

Everyone is a prospect. Initial efforts begin with the leadership first, followed by staff, volunteers, members, friends past and present, and even students.

You need to understand the power of the ask, solicit gifts in person, and ask for a specific amount.

How Much Money is Given Away Each Year?

In 2015, $373 billion was given away in the United States. Nearly $120 billion, approximately one-third, went to religious organizations, but that percentage has dropped from one-half over the years. Most novice fundraisers think that Coca-Cola or Delta might be great sources for funding, but while they are both generous donors, corporations make up only 5 percent of annual donations. Foundations give away 14 percent of the total each year. Individuals, on the other hand, donate a whopping 73 percent of charitable contributions. If you include bequests which also come from individuals, more than 80 percent of the money given away every year comes from individuals.

The moral of this story? When soliciting funds for your church, focus on individuals: church leaders, volunteers, members, friends, other staff, and students.

Types of Gifts

Churches cannot usually be supported by what comes in the collection plate alone. Therefore, most churches engage in fundraising for annual support. Capital campaigns for buildings and programs occur at most churches every five to ten years. And financially sound churches offer planned giving options to their best supporters to create an endowment for the future.

Focus on Individual Support

Churches should focus their fundraising efforts on individuals: leadership, volunteers, members, friends, other staff, and students.

Annual Gifts

Annual gifts are the lifeblood of any institution. They are typically unrestricted and used where the need is greatest. Most churches engage in member solicitations each year. Once a donor makes a gift or declines, the prospect should be pulled from solicitation until the beginning of the next fiscal year.

While individuals are the best prospects for annual gifts, corporations/businesses, foundations, or other organizations may also be solicited for annual contributions for faith-based organizations.

Typically, donors do not make annual gifts to receive something in return. Some churches do offer premiums for annual giving at certain levels. Premiums are generally offered for membership levels at varying amounts.

Corporations/businesses may choose to make annual gifts to faith-based organizations as part of their matching employee gifts program or to enhance their public presence through exhibitions or programs. Most corporations put a limit on their giving to faith-based organizations and may not contribute to churches at all.

In appreciation of generous annual contributions, a corporation will usually receive an attractive package of benefits for employees, clients, and executives.

Capital Gifts

Capital gifts are usually for bricks and mortar projects, such as a new building or renovations. Churches typically launch a new capital campaign every five years or so. (Some joke that a church is always either in a campaign, getting ready for a campaign, or finishing a campaign. It's no joke.) See **Chapter Nine** for a discussion of capital campaigns.

Endowment Gifts

If annual gifts are like a checking account where dollars come in and are spent on a regular basis,

> ### Corporate Benefits Options
>
> Depending on the level of corporate support, a benefits package may include: employee admission or membership discounts, guest passes, event discounts, invitations to special events, educational programs for employees, and annual report/website recognition.
>
> **Example**

then endowment gifts are like a savings account. Endowment dollars are never spent, but the income, or a percentage of the income, can be used for specific church programs and activities. Endowments are especially helpful in years when annual giving is down. Endowments also demonstrate the institution's strength and allow for borrowing in times of need. The best way to grow an endowment is through planned giving, which is covered in **Chapter Ten.**

Major Gifts

Major gifts can be defined as annual, capital, or endowment gifts. They are just larger than usual gifts for annual support. They may or may not be given each year, and sometimes they are just received for special purposes. Each church should seek its own definition of *major,* whether it is $1,000, $10,000, or more.

Church leaders should focus their efforts on major gift fundraising. It is the fastest way to raise more funds.

Churches need to get into the development business. Churches need to be in the habit of raising annual, capital, and endowment gifts just like other nonprofits. Churches are beginning to add their own development officers to the staff—at least making fundraising a part-time, if not a full-time, role.

Who Are Your Best Prospects?

Your best prospects are previous donors: Approximately 80 percent of the money given to your church will come from 20 percent of your donor population. A church leader's fundraising efforts should focus on individuals, usually in this order:

1. Leadership

2. Major donors

3. Volunteers

4.   Members

5.   Friends of the institution

6.   Staff

7.   Students

Corporations, foundations, and other organizations can also be solicited, but focus first on the top prospects in each individual constituency category.

Staff

Solicit all staff annually, preferably at the beginning of the fiscal year. Enlist popular staff members to solicit fellow staff members. You can hold contests for percentage giving by departments. The goal is excellent participation and only report the grand total raised. Make sure this gift opportunity is offered to employees at orientation and offer payroll deduction as an option. Corporate and foundation prospects are impressed by high levels of church leadership and staff participation.

Students

Student members are prospects and can be enlisted as donors and solicitors. They can be very persuasive and helpful. They will need a little guidance from the development team. Make sure they know the importance of the annual unrestricted appeal and are not off raising funds for benches or something the church leadership does not consider a priority.

> **Data is King**
>
> Never underestimate the power of an accurate, up-to-date database.
>
> 👍 practical tip

Visitors

All churches have guests on-site to visit worship or to attend special events. Every effort should be made to capture contact information for each. Annual solicitations can then be conducted by mail or email for these suspects as well. Research shows that people who have attended events on campus or who have been involved in some church function are more likely to contribute than those who have never been to the church.

Not all constituents are willing fundraisers, but they all have contacts and should be encouraged to share information that can be helpful to the fundraising effort for your church.

There is no such thing as no. This is our (the authors') personal mantra. Fundraising is all about getting the right person to ask the right prospect for the right amount of money for the right project at just the right time. If someone tells you no, it just means *not yet.* It means you just have one of the elements wrong. Change things up and try again. Continue to cultivate and practice good stewardship.

A Wealth of Fundraising Resources

As a church leader, you should acquaint yourself with the wealth of fundraising opportunities and considerable resources that are available.

Church leaders also have the option of participating in local, state, and regional chapters of faith-based organizations. For great access to resources and networking opportunities, find the associations nearest you.

Ethics

A word about ethics and advancement issues that affect church leaders:

In running the church, some major donors may want more of a voice in church matters. The pastor and other leaders in the church should be charged with determining worship and programs for the church. Maintain boundaries and a high level of professionalism always.

Sometimes the negatives of receiving gifts outweigh the advantages: Some artistic gifts come with too many restrictions. Examples include controversial art, real estate, and gifts with other legal and public relations issues. Be cautious and be willing to research unusual requests. Have clear giving guidelines so you can explain to donors whether their intended gifts are appropriate for your institution.

I know it is hard to imagine, but sometimes you may have to turn down a gift to your organization. Our church's school had to turn down some swamp land.

Another church was offered a piece of artwork. It was a charcoal drawing, about ten inches by ten inches, and clearly depicted a Bible story. It had been drawn by Picasso. It was authenticated (for a large fee) and many in the church were delighted and began preparing to display it. Once they realized how much it would cost to insure, properly display, and provide security, they concluded that it would not be prudent to accept it. Thoroughly research noncash gifts before accepting them.

Resources

AFP: The Association of Fundraising Professionals (AFP) is the professional association of individuals and organizations that generate philanthropic support for a wide variety of charitable institutions in 232 chapters worldwide. It requires members to comply with a Code of Ethical Principles and Standards designed to provide concrete guidelines for fundraising professionals. AFP created the Donor Bill of Rights that outlines what donors have the right to expect from charitable organizations to which they contribute. It offers a Certified Fund Raising Executive (CFRE) program to verify experience and knowledge of fundraising best practices. AFP raises awareness of philanthropy by offering programs such as National Philanthropy Day, youth programs, and awards. (*afpnet.org*)

Giving USA: Annually estimates all giving to all charitable organizations across the United States. Donations from 1.1 million registered charities are calculated with IRS records of giving by 117 million households, twelve million corporate entities, and 76,000 foundations. (*givingusa.org*)

Donor Privacy

Who in your church has access to donor records? Data should only be made available to those individuals who have a need to know. More about this topic is in **Chapter Three.**

Volunteer Management

Volunteers should be trained, and their activities supervised. Their access to confidential information should be limited. Pay special attention to church organizations offering auctions and other types of fundraisers. You need volunteers to work in campaigns and serve on the development committee, but they must be able to maintain confidentiality.

Compliance

You and your leadership team need to stay abreast of local, state, and federal laws and regulations.

Keep your church fundraising systems up to speed. Have an annual audit conducted by an outside auditor. Specific attention should be given to valuation of gifts, including auction items, real estate, and stocks. Be familiar with all the charitable solicitation laws in your jurisdiction.

Fundraising Methods by Rate of Return

There are as many solicitation methods as there are ways to communicate, but they are not created equal. By far the most powerful method of fundraising is a direct, personal ask from a top church official to an individual.

A personal ask has a 50 percent chance of success. A prospect will tell you yes or no in person. You can't ask for better odds than that. Church leaders need to devote most of their fundraising time to making requests to major donors and prospects in person.

Stewardship

The pastor's job is not just about asking. Stewardship is equally, if not more, important. The development officer will provide you with acknowledgments to sign. Add personal notes to the acknowledgments directed to people you know. We discuss stewardship in **Chapter Twelve.**

Keep a supply of birthday cards on hand. Send notes of sympathy when appropriate. Get to know your donors and their passions. Send along notes of common interest that can help strengthen the donor's relationship with the church. Send congratulations if there is a major event in the donor's life, or a church activity worthy of mention. Little things mean a lot. Staying in touch with donors on a regular basis, and not just when you want to ask them for something, will result in more gifts and larger gifts over time.

> **Special Thanks**
>
> We know of one pastor who sends a personal handwritten note to every donor, no matter the size of the gift. It takes a while, but he thinks it is worth it. It does not replace the more formal acknowledgment produced in the development office.

stories from the real world

The Importance of a Richly Detailed Prospect Database

Logically, the more prospects you have to solicit, the more donors you can engage over time. Use your sphere of influence to expand your church's prospect database. Included in this database should be all current, prior board/leadership members, volunteers, members, visitors, and event attendees. There is a tendency to overlook long-term supporters who may not have been in the church in a while. Some of your most loyal supporters may have aged and now have children or grandchildren to bring to your church.

As a general rule, if someone has ever been a donor to your church, you should not ever delete them from your solicitation rolls. You can make notations that they are inactive, if, for example, they move out of town. But keep on communicating with them through your newsletters. Make it a habit to systematically collect information about all visitors to your church. Research shows that individuals that have been to your church are more likely to support your church, if asked.

Database entries should include the contact's name, salutation, address, telephone numbers, and email address. Don't forget to add notes pertaining to the contact's key interests, philanthropic history, etc. These notes can be added by you or administrative staff.

Your church will want to solicit prospects by multiple appeal methods until they become donors or until they request to be deleted from your database. Once they become donors by some method, they can usually be renewed annually through the mail. Then you can focus your fundraising efforts on *new* major gift prospects.

Telephone Solicitations Have a One in Four Success Rate

Telephone solicitations elicit a response rate of about 25 percent. That means that, overall, you can expect about one in four prospects to "yes," one to say "no," one to say "I will consider," and one will likely be a wrong number. And with caller ID, many prospects do not even bother to answer the telephone.

After your more personal solicitations in person, more of your church leaders' fundraising time should be spent in telephoning prospects and donors than in direct mail. Volunteers, board members, and others can be engaged in raising funds by phone. Once a program has grown too large to handle internally, you can use paid telephone solicitors.

Provide callers with a telephone script or talking points. Church news, specific amount requested, and how the gift will be used are all important elements of a phone solicitation.

Callers also must be trained to have their remarks mirror the ask that may have also been in a direct mail appeal.

A combination of mail and phoning increases the response rate. If mail solicitations are sent in November, for example, make follow-up calls in December to those who have not yet responded. That will generate additional year-end gifts.

Direct Mail Can Net a One in Ten Response

Compared to personal solicitations and telephoning prospects, direct mail is the least expensive but the least effective fundraising method. You can expect a 3 to 10 percent response rate from a list of prospects who are already donors or at least familiar with your church. Some lists of less-knowledgeable prospects and nondonors or purchased lists will generate less than a 1 percent response. Direct mail is, however, the best way to reach large numbers of prospects that you will not be able to reach any other way.

Multichannel Marketing

A combination of mail and phoning increases the response rate of a solicitation. We call that multichannel marketing.

Solicitation Package Contents

Each mailing package should include a letter, a response device (pledge form with preprinted known information customized for the contact) and a return envelope. Postage-paid return envelopes increase the response rate. Make the body of the letter compelling. Include church news, a specific request, and data on why the gift is important and how it will be used. Create a sense of urgency by including deadlines such as December 31 or the fiscal year end.

Ask for a Specific Amount

An effective solicitation letter asks for a specific amount. The phrase "Would you consider a gift of xxx amount?" can be very effective. Base the amount of the request on the prior year's giving, or provide a range of options. You can also suggest the average annual fund gift or the average board gift, depending upon the audience. It is a good rule of thumb to ask for 3 to 10 percent increase over the year before. This can be calculated into a specific ask that may be different for each prospect. You may also choose to ask for a range-of-gift amounts. Some organizations only ask for an increase every three years. They simply ask for a donor to renew their annual gift at the same level of support.

The letter signer can be you (the church leader), a board member, or a volunteer. Board or development committee names can be listed on the letterhead. The idea is for the recipient to be able to make a connection with someone listed in the mailing.

The two best times of the year to mail your solicitations are the day after Thanksgiving and on or around April 15. Research shows that donors are more generous at year end/holiday times and at tax time. Donors have reviewed their finances and may be recipients of large tax refunds which they are more likely to share.

Send the letters out first class with an actual stamp if possible. First class mailings generate a better response than other classes of postage. It is preferable to hand-address the outside envelope. Include postage-paid envelopes as a response aid. Anything that makes it easier for the prospect to respond is worth the extra attention.

After six weeks, your development or business officer, or your committee members, should conduct a solicitation analysis to test responsiveness. Be sure to keep accurate, up-to-date records of all solicitation activities over time. Record the dates of solicitations, number of letters mailed, total amount raised, average gift, range of gifts, etc. This takes the guesswork out of direct mail strategy because you can adjust future mailings based on the findings.

Until your database reaches five thousand contacts, it is generally more cost-effective for mailings to be printed, addressed, and mailed from your church office. You can enlist volunteers and staff members to help stuff envelopes.

Too Much of a Good Thing

Too often inexperienced fundraisers say, "We haven't raised enough money. Let's send another mailing."

observation

Plan to send two direct mail solicitations each year (one in the spring and one in the fall) to volunteers and all constituents. Otherwise, you run the risk of losing donors since the post office only keeps forwarded mail addresses for six months. Do not mail too often or only when a goal has not been reached. Direct mail works best in conjunction with other methods of giving and as part of the overall fundraising plan.

Don't Engage Email as a Primary Solicitation Method

Think about how easy it is to send an email. It is just as easy to delete an email and it is the communication method most likely to become overused. Email can be used as a solicitation method, but very carefully, artfully, or only in conjunction with other fundraising techniques. It will likely become more important in the future and with younger member populations. Likewise, other social media will also become more helpful to church fundraising in the future.

Colleges and universities and some churches have had success with email solicitations. It is sometimes easier for volunteers to come into the church and spend thirty minutes sending personal emails to peers than it is for them to make themselves available for two hours of calls in the evening. Another benefit of email requests over direct mail requests is that emails may elicit an immediate response.

Make Giving an Option on Your Church Website

Give donors the opportunity to donate online. The church must be prepared to accept cash, checks, automatic bank drafts, and credit cards. There are costs involved with online gifts, but setup costs and fees can be offset by not having to mail pledge reminders. (There is more on this topic in **Chapter Eleven.**)

Keep online-giving-level options low. Most major gifts are solicited in person and communicated through the pastor or the development office. Remember that a large gift made online will be subject to a fee of a set percentage.

Think Twice About Special Event Fundraising

Church fundraising events are often held with the assistance of board or member volunteers. And it may be most effective to have an event to raise money for a specific program. It raises awareness at the same time it raises money. For example, when a church choir wanted to have a retreat for the choir to work on special music, it hosted an event called Choir Unleashed. It was a cabaret-style evening with desserts, coffee, and the choir singing entertaining nonsacred music. It was a big hit.

> **Raising Funds by Email**
>
> The most money I ever raised from an email solicitation was $100,000. It was an anomaly. This particular situation was one in which we knew that the prospect really cared about our institution, but he was just too busy to meet. We had the board chair send the email with a specific ask for $100,000. We had our answer in 3.5 minutes. Every now and then, it pays to take a bit of a risk.

 stories from the real world

Although events are a great way to involve a large number of prospects, event fundraising is one of the least effective methods of raising funds.

If a church is going to engage in event fundraising, pay close attention to the church calendar and be mindful of how many events are held during a given year.

Before deciding to hold a fundraising event, consider this: Is it better to ask a donor for $1,000 outright or is it better to host an event and charge $1,000 for a table of ten, netting only about $700 after expenses of about $300 are paid? In most cases, the outright ask is the better choice.

Event fundraising is also the riskiest of fundraising methods. A prime example is hosting a golf tournament that falls on a rainy day. Or your event may fall on a day that coincides with another event that your donors/prospects will attend.

When your church does host an event, revenue must be maximized. There are three ways to increase event revenue: sell more tickets, increase ticket prices, or reduce expenses. Churches should not offer complimentary tickets to individuals. Board members and other good friends of the church can and should purchase tickets in support of the event. Comp tickets should only be offered to sponsors at top giving levels. Advance planning allows time for tickets to be sold. Consideration should be given to offering a discount if tickets are purchased well in advance of the event.

If possible, announce the following year's special event and date at your event, if indeed the event is to be repeated. Some events are successful each and every year. Be sure to track annual attendance and results. Some events outlive their usefulness and need to be replaced with a new event or another fundraising method.

Gifts in Kind Can Reduce Church Expenses

Gifts in kind can go a long way in alleviating event expenses. Events held in private homes, for example, where hosts pay for food and beverages, can significantly reduce expenses for the church.

A gift in kind is a voluntary contribution of goods or services. This type gift can sometimes be converted to cash and may qualify as a charitable deduction for the person making the gift. Common gifts in kind include equipment, furniture, software, hardware, or vendor products such as food or printing.

The IRS has specific regulations regarding gifts in kind. Have a policy in place that outlines the process an employee of your organization should follow when presented with a gift-in-kind opportunity. This policy will limit the liability that may inadvertently be assumed by placing value on gifts, or by accepting a gift that does not advance the mission of your organization or cannot be readily converted to cash. It further assures that a donor will receive timely acknowledgment of a contribution.

Suggested Gifts-in-Kind Policy

Your church may accept contributions of goods or services that can be used to advance the mission of your church or may be converted readily into cash. When accepting a gift in kind, the receiver must ask the donor to provide its value.

The IRS allows an individual to deduct the full fair market value of a donated item if it is kept by your organization and used for one of its tax-exempt purposes. If the item is to be converted to cash, then the donor may claim a deduction of the cost basis or the fair market value, whichever is less. *It is the sole responsibility of the donor to determine the value of a contributed item; your church cannot assign a value to the donated item or service.*

Your organization must enter the contribution in its donor database and issue an acknowledgment to the donor. The acknowledgment will contain only a description of the contribution and will not include a statement as to the value of the contribution. It will further contain a statement as to what, if any, goods or services were given in exchange for the contribution. Your organization cannot issue an acknowledgment for contributions that cannot be used or readily converted to cash.

For gifts with values exceeding $5,000, the donor must complete IRS Form 8283 and submit the form to your organization for signature. You as the organization leader and your business officer should be the only individuals authorized to sign 8283 forms.

If your organization has signed an IRS Form 8283 and then sells, exchanges, or otherwise transfers the gift within two years from the date of the gift, your office must file a donee information return, IRS Form 8282, within 125 days of disposing of the in-kind gift. Your organization will need to advise the donor if such a transaction occurs as it may affect the charitable tax deduction for which the donor may qualify.

Beware of Gifts with Strings

There are occasions when you may decide not to accept a gift to your church. In those cases, the development office should provide a letter of regret to the potential donor.

Foundation Giving

Foundation grants can and should also be pursued. Approximately 15 percent of a church's development time should be focused on foundation funding.

Sample Sponsor Agreement

Corporate/Company Name and Organization

[Your church] is pleased to confirm a sponsorship agreement with [corporation] in support of [program/event], which will be presented [dates/location].

The [corporation] has made/agrees to make a sponsorship gift of $_____ payable on [state the agreed upon terms, i.e., one-time gift on a certain date or an initial amount followed by subsequent payments that will be completed by opening of the exhibition/event].

Sponsorship benefits are commensurate with the level of support provided and are often custom-designed to meet the [corporation's] particular marketing goals. [Your church] will provide the following benefits to the [corporation] in recognition of this support:

On-site Recognition

◆ on-site signage

◆ on-site fliers with schedule for the day

◆ verbal recognition at event

◆ event title slide

◆ title wall

Marketing/Promotion

Logo or text credit recognition in promotional and marketing materials distribute to database of approximately xx000

Paid Advertising

Logo or text credit recognition in paid advertising as available

Press and Public Relations

Text credit or verbal recognition in PR

Events/Entertaining

Opportunity to host private event, rental fee waived. Please note that all direct costs (security, housekeeping, catering, and parking) are the responsibility of the sponsor. Space available for groups from ten to three hundred.

Tickets/Catalogues/Merchandise

◆ complimentary tickets to the event; employee discount if appropriate

◆ complimentary event materials

◆ discounts on additional materials or shop purchases

◆ complimentary [level and number] tickets/materials for corporate executives

Agreed to and signed by:

Corporate Executive   Your Church Representative

Date_____   Date_____

Example

Grant/foundation proposals are typically written by the development office staff, but another staff member or volunteer may also be willing to assist. An effective proposal requires not just good writing skills, but attention to detail and knowledge of key church programs.

Equally important to the grants process is the ability to access and manage the calendar of the church leaders and key volunteers. Relationships between board members and foundation representatives greatly enhance the likely success of foundation giving opportunities. A development officer can research foundation guidelines through online resources and websites. However, unsolicited proposals or proposals sent without prior communications with foundation offices are futile. It is well worth the time to request relationship information from church leaders and friends of the church to determine who has key foundation contacts.

Once those relationships have been identified, a clear, concise communication between the foundation office and church can be accomplished. Appropriate visits with foundation staff can be arranged with key church staff and supporters, and a gift requested within foundation guidelines. Once a gift has been received, make sure it is properly and graciously acknowledged in a timely fashion and any required reports submitted by the deadlines requested.

Corporate Sponsorship

Sometimes a novice fundraiser will assume that since corporations have money, they might be willing to share with churches. Corporations are generally *not* philanthropic. Corporations by their very nature are in the profit-making business and their gifts are usually given in order to receive something. The rare exception to this might be a church's neighboring business or a business with board member, volunteer, member, or staff connection.

Faith-based events or programs are sometimes sponsored at churches. Ideally, faith-based organizations should spend only 5 percent of development efforts on corporate solicitations. For those instances where an ideal corporate connection can be made, a sample sponsorship form is provided.

A church fundraising plan should include scheduled direct mail, telephone, event, sponsorship, email, and personal solicitations. The effectiveness of all solicitations is enhanced with an accurate database and appropriate stewardship. The church leadership will need to assure that someone is designated to attend to details in the fundraising process and make sure that any and all laws are followed. The church leaders need to focus on asking for gifts in person.

To Recap

◆ Fundraising is a team effort including the church clergy, the development staff members, the lay leaders, staff, volunteers, and members.

◆ Successful fundraising requires a compelling case for support, strong leadership, and a written plan of action.

◆ The church leaders should focus on asking for major gifts in person.

◆ The overall fundraising plan should include direct mail, phoning, email, events, and corporate sponsorship and grant writing by a team of staff and/or volunteers.

◆ Good stewardship begins with an accurate database and requires speedy acknowledgments and regular personal touches.

Chapter Two

You Must Have a Compelling Case for Support

IN THIS CHAPTER

- ---→ Defining what a narrative budget is

- ---→ Why you should communicate your story through a narrative budget

- ---→ How to develop compelling materials that tell your story of how
  your church spreads the realm of God

How you develop and prepare the materials for your parishioners to review and to reflect upon during the annual pledge drive can make or break your efforts. A mission-centered budget articulates, in narrative format with graphics, photographs, and text (not just numbers), the many ministries of the church that are enabled by the gifts of parishioners.

This chapter outlines the steps to creating a budget that reflects how the money is being spent in a compelling and transparent way, yet doesn't bore your members with spreadsheets. A budget created this way reminds people of the good work that is happening in their church while reporting on the impact of their ministry and money.

In order to create this type of budget, you need cooperation from several areas: your clergy, the treasurer, each of your ministry leaders, the communication committee, and your stewardship team. Be sure to allow sufficient time to gather all you need from these areas. The first time you put this together will take the longest, but once everyone has been trained and has experienced the process, you will have a good foundation to update each year.

But what about the pages of numbers and columns that comprise the budget we work so hard on year after year? Be sure to have the line-by-line printout of the budget available for those finance types. While it will not be widely distributed, it should be ready for those who request it.

Should people give to the church? You must first reflect and review why you are a community of faith in the first place. Then, what sets you apart from the church two blocks away? How do you live out your identity as a Christian community? When people walk through the doors, what can they expect to find?

Every church is the same and every church is different. It's a bit like the old western movies, best illustrated by the movie *Rustlers Rhapsody.* In it, the main character rides into a town that is under siege from a controlling local bully. The bully has everyone cowering and scurrying to do his bidding. The newcomer seems to know everyone in the town even though he has never met them: There's the woman who owns the saloon—a tough woman who has no trouble handling the big burly drunks, but can't seem to stand up to the bully. There's the

> ### Strive to be Mission Centered
>
> A mission-centered budget reminds people of the good work that is happening in your church, and reports on the impact of their ministry and money.
>
> **observation**

sheriff, who is either on the payroll of the bully, or is new because the last sheriff was run off or killed by the bully. There's the town drunk, and so on. The same characters can be found in each town. Likewise, although each church is unique, there are some familiar characters that seem to be represented in most church communities—and it seems the similarities are even more evident when a church decides to embark upon a capital campaign. Some familiar personalities are to be expected.

In a church, you have the long-time members who don't like to try anything new—those who don't want change. Those who are afraid of being asked for money. Those who are afraid of asking for money. Those who will seek to be the center of attention. Those who will claim expertise they do not have. Those who will come from the shadows and surprise you with their leadership. And even those who will surprise you with their generosity.

So, what makes your church special? *That* is the beginning of your case for support. It is more than a mission statement, and it is not merely your vision statement. It should reflect exactly who you as a community of faith and your church's impact on the world around you.

Most churches distribute their church budget once a year at the annual meeting. It is often a shock to the average churchgoer to see how the money is allocated, and for some it is a startling realization to find out that the church must pay for the lights and water like any other property-owning entity. For those on the finance team, it is just like any other set of books that needs to be kept in balance.

Your efforts can be made or broken depending on how you develop and prepare the materials for your

> ### Tell Stories
>
> St. Francis reportedly said, "Preach Jesus, and if necessary use words." In other words, tell your story, and when necessary use numbers.
>
> **principle**

parishioners to review and to reflect upon during the annual pledge drive. A mission-centered budget articulates, in narrative format with graphics, photographs, and text (not just numbers), the many ministries of the church that are enabled by the gifts of parishioners. This approach enables you to tell your story—the ways in which your church and its ministries live out the Kingdom of God and make a difference in people's lives.

Along with aligning expenses in various ministry buckets, the narrative budget format makes clear the purpose and the mission of the parish. It answers the basic question, "Where is the money going?" while offering concrete examples of the impact of that money. If you can show where the money is going, your people can see where to give their time, talent, and treasure.

It is important to point out that this does not replace the standard budget. Nor is it a way to hide expenses. You will still have those church members who will ask for the line-by-line budget. Have it ready for when they ask for it. Then, set a time to meet with them and demonstrate how both the narrative budget and the accounting-style budget work together to tell how money is being spent. The narrative approach just does a better job of showing the impact.

Steps to Create a Narrative Budget

There are several steps to creating a narrative budget, and the first time you do this, it will require more people and effort to assemble than in subsequent years. Allow sufficient time to gather information and stories and photographs, as well as designing the brochure. Persevere and establish your own template the first time, and every year after that will be just a matter of freshening up the stories and graphs. We've included a handy worksheet to get you started in **Addendum A.**

1. Assemble a committee—see list guidelines

2. List all the ministries of your church

3. Have staff determine how their time is spent

4. Write about how people have been drawn closer to God through your ministries, using specific examples

5. Design the brochure

Step One—Assemble a Committee

The first step is to, yes, assemble a committee—this *is* a church, after all! You will want three to five people on this committee, depending on the size of your church. This is the core group who will gather, filter, and disseminate information. This group will reach out to others in the church for their expertise from time to time, but only the core group needs to be intricately involved with each step.

Identify and recruit a person who is a project manager. This is someone with great organizational and communication skills, and who can keep the project moving along. You will need someone who is good with numbers; this may be your treasurer, but it also may be a member of the finance committee or someone like a math teacher who can't commit to other, long-standing assignments. We also recommend someone who is creative—while this person might not be the one to design or edit the final brochure, your designer will need a writer and photo-gatherer to supply the basics of the information. Resist the desire to fill the committee with financial people. They tend to find numbers compelling and will not see the need to focus on your story of ministry.

Step Two—List All the Ministries of Your Church

At your first meeting, include your church secretary, parish administrator, and/or whoever has a good grasp of all the activities for your church. You will need a list of ministries and all activities that take place in your faith community.

Start by grouping them according to these six areas:

◆ Worship

◆ Christian Education/Formation

◆ Outreach

◆ Pastoral Care

◆ Parish Life/Fellowship

◆ Communications

Write each of these six areas on a separate piece of flip chart paper. Using your gathered lists and the church calendar, determine which area to place each ministry or activity. Through this exercise, you may also incorporate brainstorming to identify ministries you may have initially overlooked. It may be helpful to have a seventh piece of paper to 'park' a ministry that you have trouble placing in just one category. When the list has been sorted through a first time, consider your parked items again. It may be clearer now where you should place them.

Here are short, noninclusive descriptors of how churches we have worked with have categorized items:

◆ Worship–Activities include sermon preparation, bulletin preparation, worship planning, Sunday morning worship, special services, scheduling lay liturgical leaders, choir and music, ushers, flowers and flower guild, special items for certain services (palms, bread and wine, candles), and sound and lighting in the worship space

◆ Christian Formation/Education—Christian formation and Sunday school curricula, baptism/confirmation/marriage preparation, vacation Bible school, and safe-church training

◆ Outreach—Parish outreach events, ecumenical relationships, community ministry bulletin board, building usage (like for scouting activities), food and clothing ministries, community garden, etc.

◆ Pastoral Care—Hospital and home visits/communion, individual/crises/grief response, pastoral counseling, and other ministries that tend the sick, suffering, lonely, grieving, or dying

◆ Parish Life/Fellowship—Parish suppers, coffee hour, postcards/emails/other special notes, young-adult ministry, and the group activities for seniors, church retreats, and homecoming activities

◆ Communications—Activities dealing with the website, newsletters, printing, electronic media, social media, writers and editors, notifying media of special services and church events, and publicity for special events

Step Three—Have Staff Members Determine How Their Time Is Spent

Ask staff persons to assign a percentage of their time according to each of the six areas. A worksheet will help with the calculations. For example, your choir director might assign 90 percent of her time to worship, and 10 percent to parish life. The first category is obvious, and the second may be that your choir director also helps put on talent show with the youth group. The associate pastor's time might be divided equally among worship, pastoral care, and outreach. Once all staff members have reported in, take each person's compensation and assign the proper percentages to their categories. We recommend dividing the maintenance person's (or sexton's) piece into six equal parts. Other expenses that are not included will need to be assigned accordingly. Postage is likely for nearly all communication, wafers belong to worship, etc. There will be some expenses like utilities, debt service, or security expenses that get divided equally among the six categories.

Then, by adding up the expenses for each area, you arrive at your narrative ministry budget. We provide a sample narrative budget in **Addendum B.**

Step Four—Write about How People Have Been Drawn Closer to God Through Your Ministries, Using Specific Examples

Next, you can move on to the narrative part. This is the fun section. What did you accomplish? How many people got baptized or married? What did the kids learn in vacation Bible school, and how many kids were new to your church? Telling the story of how your church impacts others for Christ will remind the parishioners of the good work that is being done every year, every week, every day in their chosen community. Most will be astounded by the volume of ministries that make up their church's life. This can be as long or short as you have space. Tell the heartwarming stores, the fun escapades, the way you boldly reach into your community to serve the people there.

Step Five—Design the Brochure

Put all the parts together. We did not talk about where the money comes from, but this piece is pretty straightforward. Most revenue will be from pledges, plate collections, and other contributions. Your church may host a large annual fundraiser like a Christmas fair or lobsterfest, so an event like that should be a separate category. If you have an endowment and part of your annual budget comes from the interest earned, include that as a category. Take all the pieces to your designer and work to create an easy-to-read trifold booklet, or even a one-page (front and back) brochure that is used to communicate your budget. A basic example of how this could look can be found in this sample narrative budget:

The point is to get folks away from thinking about their money going to pay the electric bill and the pastor's health insurance. While some of the income does cover that, both of those items are necessary for ministry to happen. Those kinds of expenses enable the work of your church in God's realm, and to spread the Good News. This narrative budget is a tool to tell your story in a compelling manner—that without the work of your church, people will suffer and not fully know the love of God. They will come to understand that it is the whole church that matters and that each area is important.

To Recap

- ◆ Churches should strive to be mission centered.

- ◆ Define a narrative budget for how your church operates.

- ◆ Be specific on how dollars are spent.

- ◆ This budget makes asking for support of your ministries easier.

- ◆ Develop your narrative budget with simple steps that includes specific examples of how your church's ministry shares God's love.

Chapter Three

Strong Leadership is Essential

IN THIS CHAPTER

---→ As the church leader you must commit to a robust giving program

---→ What to look for when identifying and recruiting leaders

---→ Develop a leadership statement on giving

---→ Reasons why the pastor should know what the people are giving

L eadership in an annual pledge drive can take several forms. It is essential that your leadership be demonstrated to all in the congregation in several key ways. We know from years of our combined experience that people will give when the need is clearly and passionately demonstrated. As the leader of the church, you know better than anyone the stories that demonstrate that need: how people's lives have been changed by the programs of your church. You must be the chief storyteller for your congregation and passionately communicate these needs in creative and compelling ways.

Another secret to leading any fund drive in a congregation is to make it a priority of your own and make it a high-profile activity in your church. If you only give the pledge drive one Sunday of your preaching, and halfheartedly mention it during announcements, you will get what you put into it—next to nothing. However, if you visibly support your lay leaders in their ministry, and proclaim the importance of everyone taking part utilizing every tool you have at hand, your results will reflect that. Remember that your ministries will be funded—and limited—only by the financial resources collected.

You also set the giving tone for this campaign among your congregants, your lay leadership, and the staff. As the spiritual leader of the annual pledge drive, you must be the first to prayerfully examine your giving habits and respond in a sacrificial and transparent way.

Begin by undertaking a simple exercise: Take a look at your bank statement and see where your money goes. Scripturally, this can be tied to Matthew 6:21— "For where your treasure is there will your heart be also."

The next step is to incorporate your commitment to supporting the realm of God into the way you communicate and interact with others. The caveat here is to not appear boastful, but to model the commitment, the struggles, the victories, and the setbacks for your parishioners to see. Preach about your journey. Incorporate it into your blog posts or newsletter articles. Bring it up in casual conversation or at announcement time in church.

Know your number. You should know the percentage of your income that you give to furthering Kingdom work. Yes, we are talking about the tithe here. The tithe, of course, is the biblical standard of giving 10 percent of one's income to further God's realm on earth.

Those serving on the stewardship ministry team must be committed to approaching their giving to the church in a spiritual and prayerful manner. It is helpful to lead them through the Bible study on the Matthew 6:21 passage, and to give guidance on how to reflect on it over the course of several weeks. Just as your formation as a pastor matured over weeks and months and years, allow your lay leadership the freedom to undertake their journey at their pace. Don't expect an overnight conversion.

Another way to support the lay leadership of your church is to look for opportunities to send them for training that includes spiritual components of the practice of giving. Most denominations have local or regional conferences, and if you were to cross denominational lines and attend trainings that come from other traditions, you might learn from another perspective what you couldn't from just one viewpoint.

In order to have a robust pledge campaign, you must devote adequate resources to support it. There are places where this

Intentional Giving

My husband Dan and I did this exercise early in our marriage when he was still in seminary. Using an early version of money management software (this was in 1987), we entered all our financial information so that we could see the categories where our income was allotted as expenses. Not surprisingly, the majority went to rent, car payments, and insurance. What was surprising was how much we were spending on what we categorized as entertainment: eating out, movies, and other similar activities. In fact, we were shocked to see that it was the next largest category for us. Not groceries, not clothing, and, sadly, not giving to the church. It was then we realized that we had an opportunity to shift what were our clearly demonstrated priorities—spending money frivolously on ourselves—and being intentional about our spending habits. I will confess that we did not eliminate eating out with friends or going bowling. We were, however, more intentional about budgeting our money and making sure our spending priorities were first.

Once Dan and I became committed to tithing, we were intentional about the money we gave away and specific about where it went. We began a commitment to reach a tithe on our income, and that journey took about six years. Once we determined the percentage we were currently giving, we strove to increase it each year. At first, it was challenging; 1 percent of an entry level salary was a large portion to give away. Three percent, then 4 percent, then 5 percent were incrementally more challenging to add. There was some backsliding along the way, especially when a life change such as a move or a child came along. But we persevered. That spiritual discipline helped us to grow together as a couple as well as closer to God individually.

—Sarah

stories from the real world

can be done economically, but there are certain areas where you should cut no corners. Work with your church treasurer to set up a budget for your pledge drive. Initially, consider allocating 1 to 2 percent of your budget. Some money should be spent on materials (letters and postage, photocopies, etc.). Some resources will be spent on feeding your volunteers. Don't skimp on either area. Your printed materials should look professional and communicate that this is an important aspect in one's life as a Christian. Photocopies of a generic letter with a digital signature should never be sent. With software for mail merge making it easy to produce, be sure letters are personalized. They should also be individually signed. Take the time to do this. The extra effort will be rewarded by your parishioners knowing YOU signed their letter.

Volunteers are just waiting to be asked to use their professional skills in their church community. Find out who they are and recruit them. You likely have folks with the skill of layout and design. Enlist them to design your narrative budget (see **Chapter Two**). Look for a writer among those who have a blog in their professional life, or a young person with a Tumblr account. Ask them to contribute a strength of theirs to this ministry, and you may also unwittingly set them on their own journey of giving to the Kingdom of God.

How many people you have on your committee depends on the size of your congregation. If you have a small church, you can combine several positions as suits your situation. A word of caution: these roles are designed to avoid giving any current staff/administrators more work to do (as we realize they are often already overworked). There will be times, however, when a staff person may need to assist the committee members, for example, in reserving meeting space and coordinating the membership data.

Recruit a Strong Fundraising Team

Don't leave the ministry of the pledge drive and stewardship to chance. Identify, recruit, train, and support your committee members.

- *Chair/cochairs*—This position is ideally filled by two people (not spouses), so that the responsibility is shared. These individuals will schedule and preside over all committee meetings and serve as the liaison to the senior pastor.

- *Board liaison*—This key leadership role is carried out by a board member who will coordinate the activities of the committee and the board members as they are needed. Responsibilities will be to assist in recruiting members to serve on the committee, monitor progress, and report regularly to the board.

- *Congregational pledge chair/cochairs*—Also a key leadership role, their responsibilities will be to recruit congregational captains, assist in training callers, and make calls as necessary.

- *Worship liaison*—Serves as the link between the committee and the worship chairperson. This person will oversee the program items that directly impact worship services; for example, lay testimonials, lay sermon, commissioning of the committee, and hymn selection.

- *Spiritual emphasis*—This person, in some churches also known as the committee chaplain, is responsible for keeping the process grounded in prayer, in the examination of scripture, and the focus on the question, "But what is God telling us to do?" This person must understand the importance of, and be able to translate to the congregation, the spiritual dimension of being a steward. Note: Not all activity should be done by the chaplain, who should, rather, focus on coordinating the efforts.

- *Communication coordinator*—This person or persons will keep the information flowing from the committee to the people of the church. Every means available should be utilized, as appropriate for the church: printed materials (Sunday bulletin, newsletter, letters, etc.) electronic (emails and website), and social media (Facebook, Twitter, YouTube).

- *Event/ hospitality coordinator*—This is another position where it is helpful to have cochairs. The coordinator (or coordinators, if more than one) will manage planning and execution of the church-wide event or events during the pledging process. Responsibilities may include providing room arrangements, audio-visual needs, entertainment, and refreshments.

◆ *The secretary/administrator*—This person is responsible for recording meetings and activities, events, and worker progress; distributing reports of gifts and pledges; and keeping track of the timeline.

◆ *Mailing coordinator*—When a pledge program calls for items to be mailed out, this person is responsible for recruiting and supervising the team needed to complete mailings. Activities can include producing (but not writing) letters, hand-addressing or affixing mailing labels, and packet assembly.

◆ *Follow-up coordinators*—This position can be filled by two people, depending on the amount of calls to make. The coordinators recruit, train, and support a team of people who follow up on members who haven't yet responded, but are likely to. The coordinators also compile the results and postmortem evaluations.

Bringing your volunteers together to train and then to accomplish their work will be enhanced if you provide refreshments. Growing community while doing ministry is easily accomplished when a meal is shared. Jesus often ate with his disciples—he even prepared a meal or two himself! It doesn't have to be fancy. Just demonstrate that you took the time to prepare it.

Stewardship—Second Most Popular Topic

After the Kingdom of God, the next most frequent topic for Jesus to speak about was on stewardship: What we do with what we have? Jesus knew that our number one stumbling block to the Kingdom of God was our possessions.

observation

On the subject of preaching about giving, you should give it as much time as you would any other spiritual discipline. You regularly preach on the importance of prayer, worship, and service. Giving of one's financial resources is just as vital to one's spiritual wellbeing. Through parables and other teachings, Jesus demonstrated that we are to use our resources wisely and to the glory of the Father. Reminding your congregation of this aspect of their spiritual life is one of your main responsibilities as their pastor.

You can help the stewardship team by identifying and recruiting people who are spiritually grounded enough to take on this important ministry. Don't leave this job of funding the church ministries to those who volunteer; your team members should be recruited for their specific skill set.

Develop a board stewardship statement to demonstrate to the entire congregation that its leadership is committed to good financial stewardship of the church's money and of each board member's personal finances.

Your church's governing body should commit with this notion of financial giving to the church. The logical place for this group to begin is to develop a board statement on stewardship. It is an ideal way to demonstrate to the congregation that its leadership is committed to the concepts of tithing and stewardship. It also demonstrates that these concepts are spiritual matters, not financial ones. When you develop such a statement, consider how you would complete the following prompts:

◆ We believe (what you believe about God, what God created, and how we humans were to care for what God created, along with a sentence about what the tithe is).

◆ We commit ourselves (usually a statement that acknowledges the tithe and that each member agrees to work toward achieving it personally).

◆ We invite all (to join in this spiritual journey or similar language).

Once the statement is completed, send it home with each person to prayerfully consider, and then vote to adopt it at the next board meeting. Then share this journey of creating the statement with the congregation and publish it in appropriate places—bulletin boards, website, the newsletter, etc. It should be reviewed every two to three years and readdressed from scratch every five years. Also, it should be shared with each person considering service on the board prior to their joining to be sure they agree.

Why should the pastor know what people pledge? Because it reveals pastoral matters. We often have noticed that when the pastor looks through pledges for the year and notices when someone's pledge suddenly increases, it is often because something significant has happened—a spiritual awakening, a financial windfall, or something else that sparked some spiritual change or life situation. One pastor we know says that when he finds that a person's pledge doubles or triples in a year, he recruits them to teach Sunday school, to lead a committee, or to take another leadership role. He sees this increased-pledge behavior as a sign of something spiritual going on that, if harnessed, would benefit the whole congregation.

On the other end of the spectrum is when pledges drop. It's unusual to have people give five figures a year for five years in a row, then suddenly diminish to very little. What is not unusual is for that person to come in to the pastor's office and explain, "I have decreased because—and I haven't told anyone this—I lost my job," or "my child is sick with cancer," or another significant reason. In that moment, it is helpful for the pastor to respond, "I noticed and wondered if something was going on, and I'm glad you've told me." People don't find that creepy or uncomfortable; rather they find it comforting to know the pastor had noticed a change and was not upset, but appropriately concerned by the revelation. Then the pastoral relationship can begin.

> **Pledge Revelations**
>
> Knowing what people pledge often reveals pastoral matters.
>
> **observation**

The reality is that people already think the pastor knows what people pledge. Sometimes someone significantly decreases or stops pledging because of anger with the pastor; the decrease is meant to send a message. So, it behooves the pastor to already know that.

Gift Intentions: Why Lay People Should Not Decrease Their Gift When Angry

One pastor we know has said that she respects a person more who gets mad but keeps giving. It says to her that the gift comes as a spiritual response, that the gift is not quid pro quo, and that the gift is to God as a response to what has been given by God. What the consistent giving is really saying is, "I want my giving to be for spiritual reasons, not for my own personal reasons and benefits."

To Recap

- ◆ The pastor should be fully committed to a robust giving program.

- ◆ Identify, recruit, train, and support committee members.

- ◆ Have a statement that shows the leadership's commitment to giving.

- ◆ Pastors should know their members' financial giving to the church.

Chapter Four

Creating Your Written Plan for Your Annual Pledge Drive

IN THIS CHAPTER

---➤ The plan keeps you on track for success

---➤ There are many themes and approaches you can take

---➤ Plan four weeks of intense focus on funding the ministries

---➤ Identify, recruit, and train, train, train the volunteers

Your written plan for the annual pledge drive will be the document that keeps you on track from the planning stage to the final follow-up call. It includes your timeline, your program theme, leadership positions needed, training for those involved, and anticipated outcomes. Working with our sample timelines, you will learn how to sketch out each activity and assign it to the right people to do the work.

Just as in other ministries of your church, forming a committee to manage the stewardship campaign will be a natural place to start. When you identify and recruit the chair of the committee, make sure that person is committed to making this a spiritual outreach as well as a way to fund the budget. The chair should be a good project manager to make sure the team stays on track to get the job done. For a complete discussion on committee members and job descriptions, see **Chapter Three.**

Because stewardship of the gifts God has given us is a spiritual matter—not a financial matter—each meeting should be grounded in prayer and Bible study.

Regular meetings of your core committee should be scheduled at the beginning of the stewardship planning cycle. If you target October for the weeks of your main drive, then beginning your planning in February or March is not too early. Make sure that your core members put the meeting dates on their calendar and are committed to protecting them against other obligations. At first, they should be monthly, then, when you are ten weeks out from collecting pledges, move to every other week. Plan on having about ten to thirteen meetings.

A key element for laying the foundation for the work you are about to do is to wrap your efforts in prayer and scriptural reflection. They are essential to the health of each committee member. Remembering where our gifts come from, reflecting on the giver, and demonstrating gratitude will build a strong foundation for the ministry. This is a responsibility of the chaplain of the committee. Note that the chaplain can be a lay or ordained person.

One of the things you should do at the first meeting is to sketch out a timeline. A timeline is essential to keeping your program on track, keeping the process moving along, and to ensuring you go into the intense weeks of the pledge drive with as little stress and anxiety as possible.

At your first meeting of the core committee, it is helpful to arm yourself with several tools. Assign committee members the tasks of gathering up all that you need. Doing so will give everyone an easy task to accomplish before the work begins. Have copies of our timeline for each person.

Let's get started developing the timeline. Flip chart paper or a white board will be used for working out the milestones. Refreshments area a good idea, since this meeting can last one to two hours.

You should have several references at your fingertips:

❏ The church calendar with the activities that are already scheduled on it

❏ The liturgical calendar for your church year

❏ Local school calendars (private and public, primary, secondary, and college)

❏ Local annual celebrations and activities (college football, anyone?)

❏ A list of federal holidays during your pledge drive

❏ Your church's historical giving data

Now, let's create the timeline. On the flip chart paper or whiteboard, write the following milestones:

◆ Choose commitment program

◆ Recruit hosts

◆ Training dates

◆ Letter one

◆ Letter two with pledge card

◆ Stewardship education Sunday 1, 2, 3, and 4

◆ Ingathering

It will be important to be flexible in your stewardship work. Sarah worked with a church in Delray Beach, Florida, that had a very seasonal fluctuation in attendance. Most of its worshipping congregation lived primarily in the north, and came to this part of Florida for the winter. It found that the best time for its pledge drive was February. Be sure to adapt what you learn here to the culture of *your* congregation.

Before we go any further, it will be helpful for you to look at a sample fall pledge drive timeline. You'll want to refer to it as we walk you through creating *your* timeline:

St. Jude's Episcopal Church

Sample Fall Pledge Drive

Timeline

Month	Activity	Who	Due By	Done
February	Steering committee* meets: — Discuss additional members — Select Commitment Program	All* Renee & John	Feb. 15	Feb. 13
	Article due for Newsletter: Thank you for your pledge last fall—we promise to be good stewards of what you will give	Mary	Feb. 20	Feb. 15
March	Steering committee meets: — Review budget of committee — Confirm committee members — Develop timeline	All Renee & John	March 15	March 5
April	Steering committee meets: — Determine theme, develop logo. — Select Training dates — Begin recruitment of hosts/visitors (depending on Program)	All Renee & John	April 15	
	Secure Trainer for leadership training event	Renee & John Beth	April 20	
	Article due for Newsletter: When asked to serve, please say, 'Yes!'	Mary	April 20	
May	Steering committee meets: — Continue recruitment — ID other committee heads (depending on Program)	All Renee & John	May 15	
	Secure board statement	Rector/clergy	May 15	
June	Steering committee meets: — Send "Save the date" for training event to all recruited as volunteers — Develop training event	All Fred Beth	June 15	

	Article due for newsletter: Highlight visioning done by board	Mary	June 20	
July	Steering committee does not meet!			
August	Steering committee meets: — Review volunteer list — Finalize training event	All Renee & John Beth	August 15	
	Order stationery: letterhead, envelopes, thank-you notes Purchase stamps	Mary Fred	August 15	
	Rector letter sent out + Vestry statement	Rector Fred	August 20	
	Article due for Newsletter: Highlight 2-3 ministries enhanced through stewardship campaign	Mary	August 20	
Sept.	Training Event—just before or just after Labor Day	Beth	Sept. 6	
	Thank you from Chair, sent to all who attended training	Renee & John	Sept. 7	
	Steering committee meets: — Recruit follow-up committee — Track progress of visits/events (depending on Program selected)	All Renee & John	Sept. 15	
	Develop pledge card	Renee & John	Sept. 20	
	Testimonial from Parishioner (last two Sundays)	Mary coordinates	Sept. 22 Sept. 29	
	Chair letter sent out	Renee & John Fred		
	Article due for Newsletter: Here's what's ahead in Sunday school regarding stewardship education Sundays	Mary	Sept. 20	
October	Steering committee meets: — Track visits/events — Make adjustments — Train follow-up committee	All Renee & John	Oct. 15	

	Stewardship Education Sundays—2 to 3 for Adult Ed, 2 for Children & Youth	Clergy + Christian Education people	Oct. 19 Oct. 26
	Testimonial from Parishioner each Sunday (total of 4 in Oct.)	Mary Coordinates	Oct. 5 Oct. 12 Oct. 19 Oct. 26
	Preaching Sundays—2 to 3 sermons		Oct. 26 Nov. 2
	Article due for Newsletter: Testimonial by 1 or more people	Mary	Oct. 20
Nov.	Giving Thanks/Ingathering Sunday	All !!	Nov. 2
	Acknowledgment letter sent by treasurer, saying thanks	Church treasurer	As cards come in
	Notes of thanks for pledge cards sent by Co-chairs	Renee & John	As cards come in
	Article due for Newsletter: If you haven't yet turned in your pledge card, you still can & here's why it matters that you do.	Mary	Nov. 20
Dec.—Jan	Follow-up committee makes phone calls	Marshall & Ted	Begins Jan. 5
	Steering committee meets: — Postmortem evaluation for program — Dinner of Thanks for committee—CELEBRATE !!	All Renee & John	Jan. 15
	Article due for Newsletter: Here's how we did—Thank You all!	Mary	Dec. 20

*Steering committee consists of:

  Clergyperson for Stewardship (Rector should join in as needed)

  Chair people (2 ideally) (Renee & John)

  Communication person (Mary)

  Hospitality person (Beth)

  Mailing coordinator (Fred)

  Environmental coordinator (Sue)

  Follow-up committee (Marshall & Ted)

  Plus, others depending on the program chosen

Using the sample timeline as a guide, the first date to select is the day (or weekend, if your church has Saturday services) you want to gather in your pledge cards. We call that day *Ingathering Sunday*. Once you select that date, write it at the bottom of the Ingathering flip chart paper. It is best to work backward from there. Fill in the activities to accomplish, identifying which month and date it should occur.

Then assign due dates and persons responsible. Keep in mind activities in the church and community that might impact dates for the church (your pastor's vacation, local festivals), as well as those dates important to the individual responsible (travel, family weddings, sports tournaments, etc.). Be aware of the potential events that might derail the plan and schedule extra time around those, making due dates prior to any busy time. If this is your first year for having a formal pledge drive, add in some extra time to be sure you can accomplish everything without being rushed or stressed.

The budget allotted for this ministry should be addressed. Typically, a church should devote roughly three to four percent of its expected pledge income to be used for the stewardship program, which includes the annual fund drive. Knowing how much money you must work with will narrow your choices when selecting a commitment program.

Also at this first meeting, it's a good idea to review the historical data for prior years' pledge drives. Understanding details of past efforts can help to shape reasonable and measurable goals for this one. Data points to review for at least three years prior include how much was pledged, how much was collected, number of pledging units, as well as average pledge/high pledge and low pledge/mode/ median. You might also begin to keep track of who and how many people are engaged in this ministry, tracking the number of hours contributed by each.

If you have someone who is especially handy with spreadsheets, running the numbers on how individual pledges change from year to year is also helpful. The church business office may also be able to manage this part. Knowing how many people increased or decreased a pledge from one year to the next, as well as by what percentage, can be helpful to track progress of your efforts. You can and should accomplish all of this without having names attached to giving histories. If necessary, assign an account number instead of a last name to each record before sorting and pivoting. Doing so will ensure the privacy of donors.

Remember that there are several reasons you devote four weeks of intense focus on funding the ministries. One reason is to showcase how the ministries that your members funded last year have changed people's lives. Written messages from the refugee family you helped, photos from the youth mission trip, and testimonials in church during announcements are all effective ways of demonstrating your impact.

Importance of Confidentiality

You should prepare giving histories without having names attached to the records. This allows the team to work with historical data of giving without compromising confidential information. Ideally, only two or three people in a church need to know what people are giving.

watch out!

Another reason for all of this planning and activity is to get the pledge cards in the hands of the members, as well as to give contributors an easy way to return them. While the delivery method may vary from year to year—and it should—the main components of your campaign do not.

Campaign components include the narrative budget, letters, pledge cards, delivery method of pledge cards, ingathering activities, and a plan for thanking donors and volunteers

There are many types of commitment programs or approaches you can take as a hook for pledge card delivery. Resources for these can be accessed by a simple Google search of terms like *financial commitment programs, church pledge drive,* or *stewardship series,* and by researching resources from denominational websites and organizations like the Ecumenical Stewardship Center or The Episcopal Network for Stewardship. Others include Congregational Stewardship resources from the Evangelical Lutheran Church in America, the office of Stewardship and Philanthropy from the United Church of Christ, and from Discipleship Ministries of the United Methodist Church. Essential elements in each of these will include the following:

♦ Method for delivery of pledge card

♦ Committee structure with job descriptions and responsibilities with estimated time commitment

♦ Training for volunteers on committee

♦ Communicating the theme, message, ministries, testimonials, and stories

♦ Spiritual elements such as Bible study and prayer

♦ Creative ways to thank volunteers and those who have pledged

Why do you want to use a prepared commitment program? Spending a little money on these packages can save your team a lot of work and time. By having the basic tools laid out, you can use them as a template and spend your energy customizing materials instead of starting from scratch each year.

One thing you must consider when reviewing different types of commitment programs is the size of your church. Some programs are better suited for small- to medium-sized churches, while others work well in larger congregations. Smaller churches should consider programs with higher levels of personal contact, such as personal visitation programs. Trying to do this with a large church will only frustrate the committee members and inevitably leave people out—and both actions are to be avoided.

Another factor to be considered is the ease of distributing materials like the narrative budget and pledge card. If you select a program that uses small group gatherings to pass out materials, make sure you schedule enough gatherings to allow everyone

> **Commitment Programs**
>
> Commitment programs are widely available through various church resources. An internet search will provide you with many choices. Some common types include:
>
> ♦ Personal visits/every member canvass
>
> ♦ Small group gatherings
>
> ♦ Large group meal/festive gathering
>
> ♦ Note/letter-writing campaign
>
> **Example**

easy access to an event. Spreading the events out throughout the day at different times (morning, lunch, evening), at different locations (people's homes or church), and over several weeks will help people find a time to attend that is convenient for them.

Training is essential in any commitment program you choose. The kind of training we talk about here is two-fold. Part one of the training is to ensure that each volunteer understands the job to be completed and to make sure that each person has the necessary tools to accomplish the task. Part two of the training is spiritual.

The long-term goal for this ministry is to enable the conversion of your members from people who are associated with your church to living their whole lives to the glory of their Creator. Don't skimp on this part. This kind of training occurs during the Bible study at meetings and examining one's own beliefs about giving.

The result of converting a few people each year is a more committed, stable church for the long term. It is very beneficial to your church to send two to three people each year to a conference or training event. These are often held regionally or locally. It is well worth the investment to have several people come back energized and with new ideas for your strategy.

The best-kept secret of a successful commitment program may be worker training. You will find that when the workers are trained, and their expectations are managed, the work of the entire group goes more smoothly. A less-obvious benefit to worker training results in having two or three workers move from a committed pledger to a converted one. Repeat that for several years, and a shift occurs within the whole church in the attitude and practice of giving to the church.

Other considerations when comparing programs include the cost to run the program and the amount of time you have. Did you start early enough this year? Some of the choices, like the large group gathering, require that you have a large lead time to get the details in place. Others, like note writing, can be successful with less lead time. Regardless of the type, be thorough in your planning and allow for a couple of speed bumps that might delay your plan.

Be careful not to rush the process. Merely accomplishing the tasks and racing to Ingathering Sunday skips one very important element, the time for people to become engaged in a spiritual way. It is a process, and your strategy should reflect that.

If you could pass out pledge cards one Sunday and collect all of them the next Sunday, with everyone pledging ten percent of their pretax income, there would be no need for books like this one. But I suspect your church is like most all others—your members must be reminded, prodded, and coaxed to return a completed pledge. The way you deliver the cards, the sermons and corporate prayers, testimonials, narrative budget, and stories all serve to allow your congregants a way to engage this spiritual matter of giving back. Don't overlook the importance of allowing time for this to happen.

There is no one perfect type of commitment program; rather, there are several that are appropriate to each church. Once you've selected one for one year, consider a different approach for next year. It is good to rotate through two to four types because each engage your congregation in different ways—you never know what method helps someone to become converted in their financial commitment.

I know one church that did the every-member canvass every other year just to be sure that each member was reached out to periodically. Church leaders found it was a great way to clean up their records, using it to keep abreast of changes of address or marital status, for example. It also allowed an opportunity for pastoral matters to surface.

Another church selected the festive meal program to culminate its celebration of the one-hundred-year anniversary of being a parish. It was the grand finale of a yearlong recognition of its history. It could accomplish this costlier event due to its being able to draw from the budget allotted to stewardship and a portion of the budget for the anniversary events.

When to Solicit?

Change up the type of commitment program each year, rotating through several models to keep the message fresh and to not wear out your volunteers.

 practical tip

Once a commitment program has been selected, you will need to select a theme. Some programs that can be purchased will be complete with a theme, logo, sample pledge cards and letters, and other items that make it easier on the committee. Other programs do not. Selecting a theme is one of the more creative aspects for a fall pledge drive.

You can select a story from scripture as inspiration or you can come up with your own. Here are some of the themes churches have used for their pledge drives:

◆ Our Journey Together

◆ Growing in the Spirit

◆ Sow—Reap—Rejoice with Grace and Gratitude

The key is to select an image of something that resonates with your church members. Using a brainstorming technique during one early-planning meeting will allow group members to engage and to play off one another's input.

Elements of communication to your congregation during a commitment program should be strategically delivered over several weeks leading up to and including the main four-week period. You will see suggestions in the timeline of examples of what communication in the church newsletter can include. It works best to lead into the pledge drive with stories and a tone of excitement with the purpose of building your messages as the program progresses. Regular notices in the Sunday bulletin will also create awareness and build excitement.

Usually, two letters are sent. The first is from the senior pastor of the church and is an excellent way to set a spiritual foundation for the commitment program. It should speak of the pastor's own journey and commitment, and scriptural and spiritual reasons for giving to God's Kingdom. It should also reference what is to come in the next few weeks.

The second letter is from the chair or cochairs of the pledge drive. This letter also speaks to the journey and commitment of those signing the letter, as well as the process for the commitment program. It is important in this letter to include the ask. Words like, "I/We invite you to prayerfully consider joining me/us by making a pledge to . . ." These words, or similarly phrased words, must be a part of the letter. In the secular fundraising world, we call it the *call to action*.

It is rare for donors to give out of the blue. For people to give to your church, you must invite them on a journey of gratitude for what has been given, and ask that they give back a portion.

The pledge card and privacy/return envelope is often included with the second letter, along with instructions on how to return it to the church—for example, bring it to the worship service on Ingathering Sunday. Instruct that if the church member cannot be in church that day, it is to be mailed back. The exception to including the pledge card with the second letter is when there is a different delivery method prescribed by the commitment program.

Why People Give
We know that the number one reason people give is because they are asked.

important

Other pieces of the communication include the sermons (we recommend four weeks of preaching on the stewardship of God's gifts and giving back to the Kingdom of God) and testimonials. Testimonials are given by lay people, are three to four minutes long, and answer the prompt, "Why I give to my church."

We also recommend four weeks of these testimonial messages. Select people who are in the converted group to tell their story. Also, consider other characteristics—a couple and a single person, older and younger members, and even a kid—when choosing. Always preview what the testimonial givers are going to say (this is a good job for the chaplain) to be sure it stays on topic. The same person should give the same message at all services on their assigned Sunday.

Another creative way to communicate your messages is by using your website. Consider posting a video of the testimonial giver (be sure to get permission first!). Special inserts in the bulletin, a flyer that wraps around each hymnal in the pews, and bulletin board displays around the church hallways are other channels that should be used too.

> ### Get Personal
>
> I remember working with one church in East Tennessee during a worker-training session. When I asked the volunteers why they came to the session, one woman raised her hand and told me that she looks forward to the follow-up calls every year. She admitted to being anxious her first year, but she really likes to call people and "check in" on them while asking if the church can expect a pledge from them this year. She went on to say that she suspects that a few of those church members she calls now hold out their pledge, awaiting her phone call so they can chat.
>
> —Sarah
>
>  **stories from the real world**

After the final push for turning in pledge cards begins the phase of follow-up. You might try to have different people spearhead this phase, rather than those who implemented the previous phase. The primary reason for this is that this task requires fresh volunteers—those who have the energy and time to devote toward getting the pledge drive across the finish line.

The follow-up phase is where the phone calls are made to those from whom you haven't received a pledge card. Some churches elect to call only those who have pledged in previous years but haven't turned in a pledge card in this drive yet. One pastor we know made sure to announce for two Sundays prior to the follow-up calls that it was the last chance to turn in a card before the calling began. The pastor did this in a humorous way, saying that if you don't want THAT kind of call, then mail in your card on your own. It was very successful in getting more commitments and in reducing the number of calls the follow-up team had to make.

Follow-up also includes the tallying of your numbers—especially those you outlined in your plan that measure how the program did. You should then report those results. After all, you asked them to give, they did, and now the congregation can rightfully expect a report on what has been accomplished (and, if applicable, what has yet to be accomplished).

Be sure to conduct an evaluation of the entire process as soon as it is completed. Make notes of what worked well, what you should eliminate, and other ways to improve for next year.

This is also a good time to conduct a postmortem evaluation meeting to discuss all aspects of the pledge drive. All committee members should be present for this. You can use the end of this meeting to celebrate your results and to thank all the volunteers for their work.

Be sure to thank each pledger. It is appropriate for the senior pastor, the chair of the committee, or both to write a handwritten thank-you note to each person who pledged. It should not mention the amount but rather just thank the pledger for making the commitment to support the ministries. This is in addition to the official acknowledgment letter that will be sent by the business office or treasurer, which restates the pledged amount and terms (monthly, quarterly, etc.).

Finally, turn over the amount pledged to the finance committee and the board—so a budget can be put together—and take a few weeks off to recuperate. Come back ready to tackle the next campaign refreshed and more experienced!

To Recap

◆ A well-thought-out strategy will be your guiding document.

◆ The timeline helps identify what tasks need to be accomplished and who is responsible for each. It also keeps the committee members moving forward, knowing that a due date looms.

◆ Select a theme and a program that fits the size and culture of your church.

◆ Allow enough time to accomplish the tasks as well as sufficient activities and time for people to become engaged spiritually and prayerfully.

◆ Recruit as many people as necessary to accomplish the pledge drive—this varies from program to program—and be sure to train and support them.

Chapter Five

Everyone Is a Prospect

IN THIS CHAPTER

---→ Learn what defines a prospect

---→ There are generational differences evident in giving

---→ Motivations for giving are important to consider

---→ Segment your church members to be effective

There is a common myth—held especially tight in the church—that when it comes to approaching people for contributions, one size fits all. Before diving into this chapter, let's agree that one size does *not* fit all!

When fundraising for organizations, whether secular or sacred, it is important to first consider *who* you are asking for money and to approach them in a way in which they are most likely to respond. In the nonprofit world, we call it cultivation. It is a best practice of the most successful fundraisers, as well as a principle that marketers use when promoting a product.

Who are the prospects for giving to your church? The clergy, the staff, lay leaders, members, seniors, adults, young people, even children. Each category deserves its own strategy. All church members can be solicited and involved through a variety of methods, including email, mail, phone, and face-to-face, events, or group meetings. Prospects capable of giving larger amounts should be identified, cultivated, and solicited personally for maximum results.

There are some foundations and organizations that give to faith-based organizations. Include them in your fundraising plan as well as others in your community who have benefited from the good works of your congregation.

Admittedly, tailoring your appeal to your audience is a simple notion until you begin to look at the typical audience in a church. Your congregation is likely made up of many types of people of different ages and stages of life, each having different backgrounds—some with church backgrounds and some without—and who are at various points in their spiritual journey. While we are not suggesting you craft a special message for each member, we know you will get better results from your efforts if you take time to understand who the members of your congregation are and consider their reasons for giving.

Taking a page from the secular world of fundraising, translating the language can be challenging, so a few definitions of the words and phrases we use will be helpful. One word that is commonly used is *prospect*. This generally means anyone who has not yet given to your organization. Those who have an affinity, an amount of personal involvement, and who are determined to be a logical source of support are *qualified prospects*. Of course, those who have given are considered donors.

In the world of church fundraising, we use these same categories but give them different names—just like we can't seem to call the entryway of a church a lobby, but rather the vestibule. For some reason, we in the church have our own language, and unfortunately, it can be a stumbling block to those who are unchurched. You might say, ironically, that those who are seeking entry to a church for the first time are often intimidated by the foreign language many of us in churches use.

Whether you use the terms *donor*, *pledger*, *giver of record*, or even *nongiver*, knowing their affinity level to your church will help you understand how to approach them. Regardless of the names assigned, the principles of identifying, qualifying, and targeting those in your midst still apply. We will first examine your church community using generational categories and see who gives, and why. We will then look at how people are divided by their level of involvement in your church. Using these two lenses to view your congregants, it will become clear how to approach with the best results.

Start by Looking at the Differences Between the Generations

Let's start by looking at the differences between the generations. Simply put, donors in their seventies think about philanthropy differently than those in their thirties. Donors' patterns of giving change over the course of their lifetime. No matter the age or generation, the Law of Someday (see the sidebar) often gets in the way. Your job as a stewardship minister is to present the case for giving to your members in such a compelling way that they see value in giving to their church, they see it as a lifelong investment, they see the good works the church is doing in their community, and they want to be a part of it.

The Law of Someday

The *Law of Someday* explains that no matter one's age or generation, there is a fundamental belief that they will give *someday*. "We're just getting married and have new jobs," "Our children are young, and boy, are they expensive," "We've got to save for college." The excuses change but the result is the same—*someday* we will get serious about giving.

principle

The Greatest Generation

Much has been written about the oldest generation, those born between 1901-1921, and known as the greatest generation, a term made popular by journalist Tom Brokaw. This group's giving was characterized by sacrifice and the belief that giving back and sharing with others were the right things to do. Unfortunately for us now, this group is nearly extinct.

The Silent Generation

The silent generation is the group that was born approximately between 1925-1945. They were children during and formed by the Great Depression and World War II. Those in this generation value teamwork and fair play, and take their religious obligations seriously. They are also among churches' most faithful and generous members, but they, too are dying, at increasing rates. People in this group are motivated to financially support those organizations that they are committed to, and make it a part of their budget. A good approach is to send this group a letter that appeals to their sense of obligation and being a part of doing good works through their church.

Generational Giving Considerations

Generation Name	Born approximately between years
The Greatest Generation	1900 – 1924
The Silent Generation	1925 – 1945
Baby Boomers	1946 – 1964
Generation X	1965 – 1983
Millennials	1984 – 2003
Generation Z	2004 – Present

The Baby Boomers

Formed by the postwar economic boom and the notion of upward mobility are the baby boomers, who were born from 1946 to 1964. It is thought that TV advertising so influenced boomers as they were growing up that they tend not to save, but want it now and buy it now.

This group grew up with choices—the more the better. Church is just one choice they have on Sunday morning, and they view attending church as an exchange—I give you my time, you need to educate me and entertain my kids, or else we will choose another church or something other than church.

Boomers are less likely to pledge than the two older groups, and they view giving as optional, coming from the leftovers of their disposable income. They consider money a tool and ask, "What is the most I can get for it?" Consequently, this group needs to be shown the vision, not the budget.

Boomers are motivated by being a part of doing something good in their community. They are the most likely to give when asked face to face and if they understand the reasons funds are needed. The narrative budget, which was discussed in **Chapter Two,** is the main tool to reach boomers, generation Xers, and millennials.

Generation Xers

The group that has become known as generation X is made up of those born from 1965 to 1983. Generation Xers came of age as latchkey kids and children of divorce, and learned how to fend for themselves. This is the first generation where its members do not see their economic future as being brighter than their parents. They likely have little religious background and were taught little to nothing about the notion of stewardship. But those in this generation will trust the church *if* it is authentic; however, they are looking for a community, not a church. They are motivated by results and tend to give to programs, not institutions.

Millennial Generation

Formed by consumerism, global markets, and technology in every part of their lives are those that make up the millennial generation. The members of this group were born from 1984 to 2003. They are in their earning years and are open-minded and teachable. They exemplify the term *multitasking,* like teamwork, and expect recognition (they are the ones who expect to get an award for just showing up).

But people in this age range also have a global perspective. Those who attend church take their religious obligations seriously; they yearn for order hierarchy, tradition, and a calm inner world. They view money as a gift, and tend to be motivated by empathy.

These last two groups are requiring churches to rethink the pledge commitment program and even the pledge card as a response device. Reach out to these members through creative ways (use video and engage them in small-group work sessions), and demonstrate how their church has made a difference in people's lives.

Ease of Electronic Giving

Gen Xers and millennials are not likely to give by check; they are not even likely to know where their checkbook is, much less how to write a check! In fact, my kids don't have a checkbook; they use PayPal, Apple Pay, and their debit cards for most of their purchases. Churches must offer a way to give electronically—easily and securely. More about electronic giving is found in **Chapter Eleven**.

—Sarah

 stories from the real world

---

Generation Z

There is little in the body of knowledge on the last-named generational group to generalize on how its members will view giving. Growing up in a post-9/11 world, with technology available to them at a very young age, this group sees connections and relationships as a crucial part of their lives. There is anecdotal evidence that suggests church attendance of members of gen Z—at least during their young adult years—is more than double that of the millennials at the same age. This bodes well for their formation as Christian givers, *if* they are exposed to messages of good stewardship.

The children and youth of your congregation should also be included in your plan to reach everyone. You must be intentional about educating your youngest members on the importance of sharing. Philanthropy and giving are learned behaviors, and if we miss the opportunity to pass on the importance of it, our society is in for a great deal of trouble. It is well-known that the under-eighteen set has more discretionary income than any generation before it. Marketers know this well and capitalize on it. Part-time jobs, babysitting, allowances, and even money as birthday gifts are common sources of income. Teach them now to give and include them in the annual pledge drive. A $12-a-year pledge for an elementary school-aged kid is a great start to a lifetime of giving back!

Donor Motivations

Now let's look at reasons for giving from another angle. When raising money, it is helpful to understand the motivations of why people give. Donors give to a wide variety of organizations. There are approximately 1.5 million nonprofits in the United States. Some are large, national organizations like the American Red Cross, CARE, and the World Wildlife Fund. Most, however, are local or regional and have a very specific and narrow focus. Your church is one of the latter.

There is much competition for the donated dollar and you must understand who your members are and why they give. Generally, donors give for a variety of reasons.

◆ They give because they believe in the mission of the organization, and perhaps because they are involved in that mission.

◆ They give because they like knowing they are helping someone else.

◆ They give for recognition, to be remembered, or for the benefit of the community.

◆ They give as a condition of employment, because of peer pressure or for tax advantages.

People are normally not motivated by "should" and "ought." Most of us know what we should or ought to do. Often, we don't do what we should. "I should lose weight, but I don't." Simply telling people they ought to tithe does not encourage them to do so. Discovering why people give is useful in paving the way to new motivations, and can help you approach them with new ways to help them understand why giving to your church is a great idea.

By breaking up your church members into groups by how involved or connected they are, we can understand how people respond to your request for pledging. We divide the typical congregation of churchgoers into one of four main categories: Customers, Patrons, Partners, and Family.

The first category is comprised of two subgroups. The first is a subgroup of people who attend or are official members, but who give nothing to the church. They do not even reach for their wallet to throw in a dollar when the plate comes by. Those in this group may feel like the church doesn't need their money. They look around and see that the lights are on, the building is heated or cooled, the organist is there, and figure that all of this happens anyway without their contributing.

The Customer is Always Right

Roughly 20 to 40 percent of your congregation approaches giving as customers or patrons. Getting this group to give, or to give more, is challenging.

observation

However, some in this group that gives nothing are angry. They may even be angry about something that happened long, long ago, even before the current staff. Those in this group have justified to themselves that their anger is reason enough to not give. These folks think they are sending a message by withholding funds. It is unlikely that anyone has noticed, and they may even have forgotten what they were angry about.

Also in this first group are those who give only when they attend, which is only occasionally. When they do put something in the collection plate, it is usually the smallest denomination in their wallet. Essentially, those who give when they come are, in their minds, paying the price of admission. They pay because there is some good music, or because the preacher is entertaining, or their child is singing in the choir.

We call those in the first category described above, customers. Their attitude demonstrates that they are at church for reasons other than for worship. For them, the church exists to serve them, and if the service isn't up to par, they complain. They are known to say, "The sermon was too long," or "The music was boring," or "The people aren't friendly," or "The coffee is terrible." Stating these reasons allows them to withhold money and feel like they are helping the church by pointing out shortcomings. These people may even think that if these issues are resolved, they might consider giving. But often they still don't.

Patrons

The next category of your congregation can be called Patrons. In this group, you also have two main types. The Dues Payers are those who, in searching for an analogy for giving, have latched on to the concept of dues. The church, in their minds, is an organization, and organizations collect dues to be able to function. Their giving to the church translates into dues. Pledges of a dues payer tend to be in the range of $150 to $600 per year, which are like membership fees in civic and service organizations, or even a health club.

Those in this group ask, "What does it cost to belong?" Fifty dollars per month seems to be a cap on the dues-paying attitude.

The other part of the Patron group uses another familiar secular nonprofit notion called *the fair share*. People in this group look at the church budget, divide it by the number of members, and arrive at a fair-share amount. Gifts from this group will range from $400 to $1,200 per year. They seldom give more than $100 per month.

One reason this doesn't work is because not everyone can give the fair-share amount. Some make far less money and the fair share for them would be way above a tithe. For others, the fair-share amount would be a drop in the bucket. But the primary reason the fair-share notion does not work is because it is not a prayerful response to what God has blessed each of us with.

No Fair Share

Fair-share giving is not a scriptural concept. It is not a theological concept. God is not fair. Thankfully, God *is* merciful and loving.

(!) important

Patron givers care for the programs of the church. Despite being marginally committed to its future, they only think of the future in the short term. Members of this core group of givers only casually attend, although some seek to serve through the programs offered.

Interestingly, in more than fifteen years of working with churches and their annual campaign, we've noticed that the dollar amounts for giving from those in the customers group has not budged. Despite economic upturns and downturns, there is little to no fluctuation in the total dollars from this group.

It is frustrating for the stewardship committee to ask everyone in your congregation to give—even just a little—and, at the end of the pledge drive, there are still some holdouts. You should understand that those in these first two groups (customers and patrons) are motivated by external factors. These eternal factors can vary from acknowledging specific church needs (bills and payroll), or giving out of duty or obligation. Their pledges (when they do pledge) can vary from year to year and are often tied to how well they like the clergy or staff. For example, if customers like the senior pastor, they might give more; if that pastor moves on, or expresses a disliked view, customers might cut their pledges.

One Hundred Percent Giving?

Don't spend too much of your time and energy trying to achieve 100 percent participation in your pledge drive. We have *never* seen a church achieve 100 percent participation.

While it is important to include these sectors in your stewardship communications and strategy, don't expect too much from them in terms of participation and amount of giving. Despite making up the largest percentage of your members, the patrons and customer sectors—combined—account for only about 35 percent of what is given to a church. Reach out to this group, include it in all activities, but don't spend too much of your time chasing down pledge cards that are not likely to be turned in. As the saying goes: Never try to teach a pig to sing; it's a waste of your time and it annoys the pig!

When giving is motivated by external factors, the church is left vulnerable to shifting feelings and opinions. Even more importantly, external factors leave the church in a maintenance mode, unable to move beyond the status quo to vision, mission, and action.

Everyone is a Prospect

Changing behaviors requires far more than telling people they "ought" to give, or give more. Real change occurs only when motivations are shifted from external to internal. This shift is part of the mystery of God working in our lives. When doing stewardship education, information is helpful, but only up to a point. Our hopes and desires often exceed our ability to perform. To paraphrase Paul in Romans, we do not do the good we want to do.

To move from maintenance to mission, or to move from external motivations to internal ones, requires stepping out in faith—crossing the Red Sea of conversion. That conversion is a process that can occur over one stewardship drive or over many years. More about that conversion will come later in this chapter.

Partners

The next sector of givers can be called Partners. As much of 10 to 15 percent of your church is comprised of this type. They are characterized by percentage giving, which includes tithers. We refer to these as partners because they are 'partners with Christ' in the mission of the church.

Those in this sector are the most likely to have sat down with paper and pencil to figure out what percentage of their income they are giving to expand the work of the Kingdom. Many who can be defined as percentage givers not only know their number, but are working toward giving a tithe—a full 10 percent—of their income.

Everyone who gives is a percentage giver, but if the motivation to give is not an intentional percentage, they are not considered percentage givers.

The tithers intentionally give at least 10 percent of their annual income for God's work in the world. The word *tithe* is mentioned sixty-seven times in the Bible; therefore, it is considered by most denominations to be the minimum standard of giving. Yet only a small percentage of your congregants give a full tithe.

Family

There is one more sector in this categorization of the types of givers: Family. They can also be described as Joyful Givers. Although all giving can be joyful, some receive the spiritual gift of generosity. These people—a mere 1 to 3 percent of those in your church—understand fully the theological notion of being a steward of God's gifts, and tend to live their lives with care and generosity. Joyful giving extends to every area of life. The idea of two worlds, sacred and secular, falls away and the worlds become one. In looking for ways to give, the joyful giver feels like a grandparent wanting to give gifts to grandchildren.

When you combine the Partner and Family sectors, they will make up only 10 to 15 percent of your church membership. However, they also account for approximately 65 to 75 percent of the total amount given. The amount they give is an intentional percentage of income. People in this group have spent time prayerfully considering the role of the church in their lives and want to give as an outward and visible sign of their inward and spiritual grace. Giving for them is more on a sacramental level.

The members in the Partner and Family sectors are motivated by internal factors. They give in response to God's blessings, and with gratitude. They want to further the mission of the church and do so by

> ### Joyful Giving
>
> A joyful giver will be giving 10 percent—or more—to further God's realm on earth. As church fundraisers, you must acknowledge that some of that may go to other organizations that the donor feels are worthy of being in that category.
>
>
> important

being faithful to their need to give. This last reason—a need to give—is perhaps what denoted the clearest distinction between this sector of givers and the Patrons and Customers.

Remember that Red Sea of conversion? That's where this comes in. Moving from one set of motivators (external) to the other set of motivators (internal) is a huge step. Conversion is a leap that calls for risk and surrender. For those of us on a spiritual journey, there are liminal moments when we see things differently and reach a turning point, and then come to a new understanding. The Greek word *metanoia* has to do with coming to wholeness of mind or having a new insight. It is a shift that occurs so profoundly that we can never go back.

Stewardship Opportunities

Your job as part of the stewardship committee is to provide opportunities for people to engage scripture and prayer in their everyday lives so that these moments are possible. The moments are directed by God; we just provide the opportunity for them to happen.

Send your members giving statements on a regular basis. These reminders will help them keep track of their giving and help them budget their pledge throughout the year.

Identify Your Target Market

A basic marketing principle is to identify your target market. When you apply this concept to fundraising, we call it segmentation.

To effectively reach your target market, you should look at your church's membership based on three things. The first two are their generational characteristics as well as their reasons or motivations for giving, which were described earlier in this chapter. The third is their consistency in giving to your church. Those who give every year need only to be kept current with how your ministries are flourishing. Those who have lapses in their giving may need a more robust educational type of communication to get them reengaged.

By treating people differently, you are recognizing that they have different needs. In the fundraising world, there are two terms for people who give occasionally to an organization—those who have lapses in their giving history: LYBUNT and SYBUNT. They are acronyms for Last Year But Unfortunately Not This (year), and Some Years But Unfortunately Not This (year).

For these groups, keep in mind that it is probably less about your mission or ministry and more about their personal circumstances, whether just forgetfulness or fluctuations in cash flow. This is one reason we recommend the use of giving statements. These are best if sent regularly to those who have made a pledge, so that the entire year doesn't slip by without their giving to the church.

We have covered giving by individuals and families, but churches can also look to foundations, businesses, and their community as a source of revenue. Keep in mind, however, that these three groups will only represent a small part of your income. Plan your strategy and time accordingly.

Foundations that are the most likely to give to a church are family foundations. You must know your members well to find out if they have a family foundation or donor advised fund because they are not often apparent. Businesses that give to churches usually only do so for a special event or a special project. Businesses are less likely to give a contribution to your church's annual fund and more likely to sponsor an event or project (like a local nursery sponsoring the church's new landscaping). Community members and groups are another potential source of additional revenue. Apart from building usage fees for groups to use your facility, these are also most likely to be limited to special occasions.

Realistic Expectations

Keep your expectations of giving from outside groups realistic. One church in Virginia that Sarah worked with was over three hundred years old. It had an historical organization that had been established for nearly half a century to help maintain the church building. On one occasion, this society moved the church several miles inland from the Chesapeake Bay to keep it from being threatened by the elements. When it came time for a new roof, however, the church asked the society to contribute. Although the group made a gift to the fund, it was not nearly as much as the church had hoped. To keep the relationship strong, and to reduce the likelihood of this happening, be sure to continuously cultivate and communicate strategically all throughout the process.

To Recap

◆ Everyone who attends your church for worship or other activities is a potential giver.

◆ When you break down your members into generations, you understand how they view giving and their level of loyalty to your church.

◆ Even across generations, internally motivated donors tend to give at higher levels than those who are externally motivated.

◆ Segmenting your church and targeting your letters of communication will yield the best results.

Chapter Six

The Spiritual Side of Giving: Churches Have an Advantage

IN THIS CHAPTER

---➤ Scripture is packed with tips for your relationship to money

---➤ You have a captive audience every Sunday

---➤ Examine your own relationship to money to understand how to be a better steward of it

Whenever we (the authors) begin teaching about the theological notion of stewardship to a group of church people, we find it is best to start by taking a survey of those in the room. We announce that there will be a one-question pop quiz, and everyone who agrees with the statement should raise their hands.

We assure them that this will be the only question that we want a public response to: "Raise your hand if you agree with this statement." At this point every eye is on us while we raise our own hands to demonstrate. Every ear is tuned in for the question. And we always get the sense that there are those who are eagerly looking forward to keeping their hand on the table, just to be contrary.

But after a pause, one of us states the phrase, "Raise your hand if you agree with this: I believe in God." After several seconds, all hands are indeed in the air. We thank them and tell them that we are glad that they have responded that way because if not, their pastor needs to have a sidebar conversation with them before we go any further. Usually a bit of nervous laughter follows this. You see, if we can get them to agree on that one starting place—*I believe in God*—then we can all get to the place of understanding that we have a Christian responsibility to be good stewards of God's gifts.

You are a member of a community of faith, and it should be expected that God and the Bible would be a part of this conversation. Contrary to some notions, using scripture as a basis for fundraising in a church is not manipulative; it is used for several fundamental reasons. Foremost, it models how we should approach our individual relationship to money. In the New Testament, Jesus told many stories about people and their relationship to money. In fact, except for the Kingdom of God, Jesus talked about money more than any other subject! These examples were included in scripture for us to learn about ourselves

Biblical Stewardship

Stewardship is all that I do, all that I am, after I say, *I believe.*

through them. Use them throughout your pledge drive so that people can see that the Bible really does speak to us today.

If you believe in God, and are still reading, we can start our walk-through scripture with page one in Genesis: "In the beginning, God created the heavens and the earth." This is hopefully a familiar passage to you. God is Creator of all, and is therefore the owner of all. At this point in the class, we write, on the left-hand side of the board, suggestions from the participants of all the things that God created. Usually, the list includes people, various animals, trees and flowers, the sun, moon, stars, and so on. Sometimes people will include church, time, health, marriage, the Bible, wealth, and other broader items and concepts. When this happens, we know they are beginning to get the hang of it.

We find out further in the first chapter of Genesis that God delegates the management of creation to the humans (who were created in God's image). God gives it to us and we become stewards—keepers or managers—of all that God created. It is our task as stewards to care for the gifts that God has entrusted to us. We are to be grateful for those gifts and care for them in such a way as to be able to enjoy them and then pass them on.

Stewardship is the work of the church. The work or mission of the church is taking what we have been given and using it to the glory of God.

So, we, in turn, offer these same gifts back to God. A familiar phrase from 1 Chronicles 29 states that all things come from God, and from that, we give back to God. At this point in the class, we turn back to the board and write on the right-hand side all the things we give back to God. People begin to suggest gifts you would expect, such as time, talent, and money. But this time, they more readily list specific gifts like flower arranging, being a Sunday school teacher, organizing the food pantry ministry, a specific pet, prayer, even their own children. Understanding that it is a continuous loop—God creates, God gives, we care for the gifts and are so grateful for them that we give back—is the basic principle of what it means to be a good steward.

Keeper of the Sty

Stewardship is the management or caretaking of something that belongs to another. The sty-ward of centuries ago was the keeper of the sty, and who was employed by the owner. Similarly, the wine steward is responsible for the stock of wine owned by the restaurateur.

Which brings us to the one question everyone always wants answered. And at the same time, people know they are not going to like the answer to this burning question: How much? How much should I give to the church? One thing we have witnessed is that how much people give directly correlates to their spiritual health.

The Tithe

At many of the places we go, there is a lack of understanding about the word *tithe*. Traditionally, it means giving back 10 percent of the first fruits of labor. Since few of us live in a strictly agrarian or barter economy anymore, in our current day we understand this to mean money straight from our paycheck.

You need only to review Exodus 23 to see how firmly imbedded giving back is in one's relationship with God. This section of Exodus speaks of the choicest of the fruits, the first fruits of your labor; it says that your gift should be the best you have to give, and comes off the top—not left over after taxes, bills, and indulgences. This usually makes people squirm.

God wants 10 percent of the money that I make? For what?

Well, we are asked to make these gifts to the glory of God and to further the Kingdom of Heaven. But the reality is that God doesn't need our money. We as Christians give because we have a spiritual need to give—in fact, to give back to God. We give as a reminder of what we have been given, out of gratitude.

God Loves a Cheerful Giver

Remembering the words from 2 Corinthians 9, we see that God loves a cheerful giver. Becoming a cheerful giver is becoming the person who understands just how much we have been given—everything. We have been given the greatest gift of all—God's Son, who lived and died and rose from the dead, who knows us as well as all our shortcomings—and forgives us anyway. Through God we have been given life. Through the gift of his Son we have been forgiven. And through that gift of forgiveness we are offered eternal life. It is based on the certainty of this Good News that we learn to freely share of our gifts, and learn, too, that sharing becomes joyful.

Knowing your own relationship to money will help you become a good steward of it. Some self-examination of how you view it will help. What are your earliest memories of money? Did your family talk about it openly, or just say there's not enough? How do you handle the money you earn—do you take advantage of the tax deferment and put some away in a retirement account while leaving some in a more accessible savings account? Or does it all get spent every month? Do you share any of it? With whom? How often? Do you view it as a tool or as a necessary evil, never having quite enough? What do you own and what owns you?

How Do You Relate to Money?

We will never be able to ask for money if we do not know how we ourselves relate to money.

—Henri J.M. Nouwen

It's too bad that money is such a taboo subject in our culture. It is rude to ask someone how much they make, and it is a more forbidden topic than politics or religion. Once you comprehend more fully your own relationship to money, then you are better able to help guide others on their journey toward understanding.

Another advantage churches have is that of a voluntarily captive audience. They have chosen to come together in search of guidance, teaching, and formation. Each Sunday, your members are gathered for worship and Sunday school. Use that time wisely throughout the year. Your messages of stewardship for what we have been given should not be restricted to a four-week pledge drive. In fact, that is the opposite of what you should be doing. Incorporating these messages in the life of your congregation all year long will allow people to more readily grasp the notion of being a steward.

While the topic of year-round stewardship is more fully discussed in **Chapter Twelve,** here we will examine ways of incorporating messages on giving into Sunday mornings.

Preaching is, of course, the most obvious place to deliver messages of what good stewardship looks like. The Gospels alone offer more than a dozen opportunities to illustrate it. One of our favorite stewardship passages comes not from a Gospel, but from Acts 4:32.

Peter and John had just been released from prison when they return to their friends and relate their experience. Together, they pray for the strength and the abilities to continue their ministry. The group's prayer is answered rather boldly by an earthquake and by being filled with the Holy Spirit. Then we hear about how they lived in community: No one claimed ownership of any possessions, but everything they owned was held in common. The members of this group who owned land sold it and offered the proceeds for the common good. It was laid at the apostles' feet and distributed to each as any had need.

Secular Stewardship

In the secular fundraising world, the term *stewardship* refers to the actions the people of the organization take to ensure the relationships with their donors are current. The development professionals must make sure they communicate appropriately and often so that the donor's ties to them remain strong.

Discomfort about the Tithe

Often, as we teach a new group about stewardship, there is discomfort. The closer we get to the subject of the tithe being a standard of Christian giving, the more people will become uncomfortable. They begin to push back. Often, someone will ask this question, "I don't remember any of this in the New Testament. When did Jesus talk about the tithe as the Christian standard of giving?" It is at this point that the story becomes so helpful. The question is accurately stated. Although Jesus spent a surprising amount of time addressing what we do with our money and resources, the tithe was not a leading topic when He spoke on the matter. The story highlights a more surprising standard Jesus used: *everything*. We help people push though their discomfort by reminding them there are two standards of generosity in scripture. One is the tithe. The other is everything. They are free to choose either one.

The following table includes some of the scriptural references from the Gospels that have a stewardship-themed story.

Story	Scripture Reference
Parable of the talents	Matthew 25: 14-30
Widow's mites	Mark 12: 41/ Luke 21: 1-4
Parable of the rich young ruler (give away all that you have)	Luke 18: 18-30
Parable of the good Samaritan (caring for others)	Luke 10: 25-37
Parable of the two debtors	Luke 7: 36-50
The ten lepers (gratitude)	Luke 17: 11-19
For where your treasure is, there will be your heart also	Matthew 6:21
The responsibility of giving	Luke 12: 48
Give and it will be given to you . . . a good measure, pressed down . . .	Luke 6: 38

Other than through preaching and Sunday school or formation classes, there are ways to incorporate notions of giving in your worship service. Carefully select the hymns for the day so that they speak to the same message as heard in Bible readings or the theme in the sermon. You can craft or edit various prayers for use throughout your service. Utilize the offering as an act of worship and give it its full due—don't bypass the choir. Instead, make sure the offering of one's possessions to the glory of God is recognized as an outward and spiritual act.

The worship service is an excellent time to lift up the ministry of the stewardship committee. At the beginning of their work, set aside time during your church services to commission this group for their ministry. This signals to them and to the rest of the congregation that it is an important part of the church life.

Plan your Sunday school offerings to complement your pledge drive. Educating your church members is an obvious way to lift up the importance of this ministry. It also serves to allow people the opportunity to interact with the theology of stewardship over a course of several weeks. This serves to help parishioners make their own decisions about giving, offering guidance and suggestions in a way that allows them to fully embrace their role as a steward. You have learned that we are all stewards; some know what that means and strive to be a good steward of the gifts we have been given. Your job on this ministry team is to provide enough interactions with the concept of managing our gifts so that people want to become good stewards.

Combine each of these activities during the intensive four-week pledge drive period, but also throughout the year as appropriate. Remember that since the average member considers regular attendance to be twice a month, you should repeat your messages (in different ways) over several weeks.

Stewardship Over Time

If you want your members to fully grasp what it means to be a good steward, you must give them many opportunities to interact with the ideas of generosity and where their gifts come from. Don't expect them to have a conversion in a month; this transformation usually takes place over months or even years.

To Recap

◆ Who among us would not want the recipients of our gifts to use them as we intended when we made the gift?

◆ In Christian stewardship, and as we have seen at the beginning of this chapter, God is the giver, the donor. The job of the Christian is not to begrudgingly discern how much we will give away, but instead to awaken ourselves to the reality that God is the donor. We are the gift. Discerning God's intent for how the gift is used in the world is at the very heart of what we are called to do as people of faith.

◆ Scripture is written to teach, to model, and to guide our lives; it is useful to demonstrate the principles of giving and Christian stewardship.

◆ When your church members make themselves available to you, use that opportunity to teach about the importance to their spiritual lives of giving, just as you would teach about prayer and worship.

◆ Begin by examining your relationship to money and consider how your life reflects the principles of good stewardship.

Chapter Seven

Operational Funds Have Less Donor Appeal, but They are Essential

IN THIS CHAPTER

- ---→ The importance of the annual appeal in your church

- ---→ Elements to include in your annual campaign

- ---→ Membership is critical to church fundraising

- ---→ The importance of the annual report

Annual gifts are the lifeblood of any church. They pay the salaries and maintenance and all that it actually costs to run the church. Typically, unrestricted, annual funds are used where the need is greatest. Annual funds do not finance new buildings. Annual funds do not create endowments. Annual funds do not usually provide enough resources to grow an institution. Let's face it; it is just not as sexy to raise money to pay the light bill as it is to build a building.

Of all campaigns, annual campaigns are the least cost effective, especially if you are in the start-up phase. Well-established annual funds with a loyal donor base are less expensive. With new initiatives, the cost to educate and acquire a new donor may equal the amount of money raised in year one. The cost of raising a donor dollar is substantially less than raising a nondonor dollar. Once a donor makes a first gift, that same donor is more likely to return as a donor and become an annual donor.

Each year the development/stewardship team must motivate last year's annual donors to give again, and give at a higher average gift. They must also try to attract new gifts and reattract lapsed donors.

When to Launch an Annual Campaign

How do you know when you are ready for successful annual fundraising? Here's a checklist of questions to answer:

❑ How long has your church been in existence?

❑ What percentage of the annual budget is covered by what comes in the offering plate and other sources of funds?

❑ Do you have a written plan for the church?

❑ Have the staff and church leadership identified the church's immediate and long-range needs (with accompanying costs) that justify fundraising?

❑ Is there a written case statement that describes those needs?

❑ Is there a written plan for annual fundraising and has it been approved by the church leadership?

Sometimes it is advantageous for a church to conduct a development assessment. In an assessment, usually an outside observer reviews past fundraising activities and makes recommendations for improvements. An analysis of where your gifts come from, what percentage of the budget is provided by the annual campaign, and the costs per dollar raised are all measured.

Plan in Advance

Plan ahead! If and when you are considering initiating an annual campaign, it is essential to craft a plan. Successful annual fundraising drives should be planned at least one year in advance. The annual campaign timeline must allow for the following:

◆ Church leadership approval of the annual fundraising plan

◆ Donor research and identification

◆ Solicitation by categories

◆ Special events

◆ Follow-up to solicitations

◆ Appropriate acknowledgment and stewardship

Setting the Annual Campaign Goal and Securing Leadership Commitment

If you have established that an annual stewardship campaign is needed based on a well-documented assessment of operating needs, set a conservative dollar goal for your annual campaign. This dollar goal must be fully justified and obtainable. If not, the church may need to adjust the budget!

You can set a goal that closes the gap between offerings and the cost to run the church. You can base an annual campaign goal based on last year's fundraising totals with a little bit extra percentage for this year. You must consider, however, if there are any one-time gifts that will be lost. Is there any possible impact from a special event or occasion that will not be repeated? There will likely be new donors and new members, and therefore new prospects. There may also be outside factors that affect a possible campaign: news, the economy, politics, scandal, etc.

to-do lists

Calculating Your Goal

Let's assume your objective is to increase the annual campaign by 10 percent over the previous year. If you raised $250,000 last year, the increase would be 10 percent x $250,000, or $25,000. The new goal would be $250,000 plus $25,000, for a total of $275,000.

However, if there was a one-time gift last year of $25,000 that will be lost, and you normally have 1 percent gift attrition ($2,500), your starting point would be $222,500. You will actually need $52,500 in new monies, not $25,000, to reach your new goal for the year. In reality, you need a 21 percent increase to reach goal. Is a 21 percent increase in one year really attainable?

Leadership Giving

Once your annual campaign goal is determined, you must then obtain buy-in as well as a pledge of full support from key church leadership. The board leadership and the ministerial staff must fully embrace the annual campaign. One-hundred-percent participation of the church leadership in the annual campaign is expected. That support must be formally demonstrated early and communicated publicly throughout the annual campaign.

In your planning, add some time to create a statement of what your leadership believes about financial giving to the church, its scriptural basis, and how it is reflected in the actions of the church leadership. See **Chapter Three** on Leadership for a sample statement.

Once the overall dollar goal is approved and committed to by top leadership, realistic and obtainable sub goals for each constituent group must be set based on prior giving and reasonable incremental increases. All of the goals for the various constituency groups should total more than the amount needed in the annual campaign. That will allow for a bit of a cushion in case one or more groups do not meet their goals.

A budget for the annual campaign must also be established and approved. For most churches, the annual campaign budget should be 10 to 25 percent of the revenue raised in annual support. The budget must cover salaries, printing (stationery, brochures, annual report, reply cards, and envelopes), special events, premiums, recognition, phonathons, travel (if needed), and ever-increasing postage costs.

Establish the Annual Campaign Chair and Committee

It is wise for churches to enlist an overall annual stewardship volunteer chair. This key leader is usually a board member and a regular contributor to the annual campaign at a leadership level. The chair's primary task will be to engage the other constituency groups and assist them in reaching their respective goals. On the following page is a chart of the suggested hierarchy of the annual campaign committee.

Annual Campaign

The annual campaign chair should be a major donor with visibility and stature in the church community. This individual will serve as chief spokesperson for the annual campaign, sign appeals, identify

Be Creative

One church we know used its word-processing program to create special letterhead for its annual campaign. One volunteer created the logo based on the church theme for the year, and the committee names were added. The following year, the design was changed to include the names of all the ministries around the outside margins, creating a border.

stories from
the real world

Chart of the Suggested Hierarchy of the Annual Campaign Committee

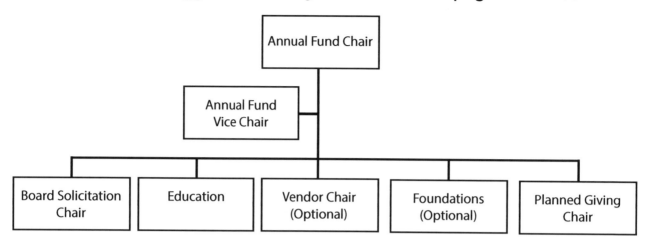

and cultivate donors, and personally call on a short list of prospects. It is customary to list each of these volunteer names on church/campaign letterhead for solicitations and acknowledgments.

The annual campaign vice-chair assists the chair and is in training to chair the annual campaign the following year.

These volunteers should be recruited by the development staffer and/or the annual campaign chair. Each volunteer should be trained in how to ask for gifts in person. Each constituency/subgroup chair must then recruit and train additional volunteers to serve on subcommittees who will solicit annual campaign donations from each subgroup of their constituency.

The Annual Fundraising Plan

The annual campaign plays a central role in the total church budget. It is the building block upon which other funding rests. So, whether you have a fledgling annual campaign, your fund has reached a plateau, or you just need ideas to motivate staff and volunteers, your church needs an annual fundraising plan. Use the following outline as your starting point:

Annual Fundraising Outline

I. Background

II. Objectives

III. Goals/Strategy

  A. Underlying Philosophy

  B. Defining the Prospect Pool

  C. Sequential Fundraising

  D. Personal Solicitations

  E. Solicitation of the Church Leadership

  F. Strategic Marketing Tools

The Nuts and Bolts of Acquiring Annual Campaign Donations

Fortunately, raising annual operating funds is not rocket science. The annual fundraising program can be divided by giving level into logical segments. This will allow you, the clergy, or other designated individuals to focus on a few top donors and staff, and other volunteers can give attention to the rest.

Acquiring Major Gifts

The success of your annual fundraising is largely dependent upon your success in acquiring major gifts.

As much as half of your goal could be expected to come in the form of a major gift. We recommend these steps:

◆ Define what a major gift is for your organization.

◆ Develop a range-of-gifts table.

◆ Identify major-donor prospects, segmenting them into renewing or new donors.

◆ Craft an individual strategy for each major gift prospect. (Who should solicit and for what amount?)

◆ Assign five prospects to each solicitor.

◆ Secure 100 percent participation (in unrestricted dollars) from the board.

◆ Secure a challenge gift/fund of at least $5,000. A challenge issued by a church leader or other donor will motivate donors to give more because their gifts will be matched.

◆ Personally cultivate and solicit donors/prospects.

◆ Schedule personal solicitation visits with each major annual prospect.

Giving Levels

It is standard practice for nonprofits to establish giving levels or donor clubs to encourage giving at specific levels. Churches should consider this technique as well. Donors are incentivized to give at the level of their peers. A suggested breakdown might be as follows:

Annual Campaign Giving Clubs

$5,000	[Giving Club Name]
$2,500–$4,999	[Giving Club Name]
$1,000–$2,499	[Giving Club Name]
$500–$999	[Giving Club Name]
$250–$499	[Giving Club Name]
$100–$249	[Giving Club Name]

important

Solicit Everyone and Establish Giving Levels

Individuals are the best prospects for annual gifts. All constituents in the church community should be solicited for annual gifts every year until a response is received. Once a donor makes a gift (or declines), pull the prospect from solicitation until the beginning of the next fiscal year.

Make it a practice to thank each donor within forty-eight hours of receipt of the gift. At the end of the campaign, donors and volunteers will also be thanked publicly in the annual report or newsletter.

Seek Tribute Gifts

Offer donors the opportunity to contribute to the church in honor of, or in memory of, a friend or loved one.

Gifts in Honor

A donor can celebrate holidays, birthdays, anniversaries, or any occasion with a gift to the church in honor of a colleague, friend, or family member. An honor gift is a unique way to recognize loved ones in a meaningful, creative way.

Gifts in Memory

A memorial gift celebrates the life of a friend or a loved one. The gift might be in appreciation of the loved one's devotion to faith.

List tribute-gift options:

- ◆ In annual appeals

- ◆ In special event mailings

- ◆ On the website

Personally recognize gifts of $25 or more with a letter to the family of the recipient. Tribute gifts, while handled specially, can go to the annual operating budget.

Pursue Foundation Gifts

Corporations will likely not contribute to faith-based organizations. However, there are foundations set up by believers that sometimes make annual contributions to churches within similar denominations. To thank the foundation, a church may offer event invitations or educational program opportunities for employees and annual report/ website recognition.

Make it Easy to Give

- ◆ Give volunteers and colleagues an annual campaign calendar so they can follow progress and support the program.

- ◆ Offer payroll deduction as a giving option for staff. Include annual campaign information and a response device in new employee orientation packets.

- ◆ Offer electronic funds transfer as a giving option for church members. Larger gifts are possible if payments are spread over time.

- ◆ Offer a super-easy online giving option. Make sure it works properly. See **Chapter Eleven** on innovations in faith-based giving.

- ◆ Accept VISA/MasterCard for gift payments. Make it painless for donors.

- ◆ Include memorial and tribute-giving options in annual campaign materials. This works especially well for additional funds for flowers at Christmas and Easter.

 practical tip

Compelling Annual Campaign Communication

To be effective, the annual fundraising letter must be personal and specific. It should be written by the campaign chair and be from the heart. Address the letter to an individual, not the masses. Consider starting the letter with a personal story that will hook the reader's interest. Avoid falling back on writing about the weather or the change of seasons. Avoid the theme of *we need your money*.

In the body of the letter, tell the reader the dollar goal of the annual campaign and be specific about how the dollars raised will be used.

Make sure to ask for a specific amount; this is often done in the postscript. If it is a new prospect, you can suggest the church's last year's average annual gift, or offer a range that covers the average gift.

Make it easy for the reader to respond. Provide a return envelope and preprinted pledge card. Address the reply envelope to a specific person at your church. Do not use postcards in lieu of letters because they provide no opportunity for a response.

Enhance the outer envelope with a tag line such as *a message from the pastor*.

Use first-class postage and hand-address for the outgoing mailings whenever possible. It will be more likely to be opened.

Sample Appeal Letter

Dear [first name]:

I hope you and your family are having a relaxing summer. It seems like only yesterday we were making plans for the summer, and now it is almost time to begin another church year.

Thank you for your past support of [name of church]. As a member of the board of trustees, it is important that we continue to set an example for volunteers, staff, members, and foundations by contributing to the fundraising efforts here at [name of church].

I am writing today to ask you to join me in making your contribution to the annual campaign. Your leadership gift at specific amount will allow your membership in the roundtable of gift clubs at the XYZ Club level. Our goal is to raise $800,000 and to increase the number of donors in the XYZ Club.

As you know, the annual campaign is the most vital fundraising effort at the church. You should also be aware that one of the main functions of the annual campaign is to keep our programs running smoothly. Your tax-deductible gift to the annual campaign makes a huge difference. Your gift directly impacts our ability to serve our members and the community here and abroad.

Enclosed, please find a brochure with more details about our programs and needs and a pledge card. Please respond by the end of the month so that we can bless the pledge cards during our worship on Ingathering Sunday, [month date], and conclude the annual appeal by the close of the fiscal year.

Thank you for all you do for [name of church]. Your commitment to the success of the church makes [name of church] what it is today and allows us to do the Lord's work.

Sincerely,

[signature]

Annual Campaign Chair

Example

Membership

Participating in the annual campaign is expected of all church members, if not at the tithe level, at least at some level. All new-member orientations should delineate expectations.

To grow its membership base, a church must always be creating convincing appeals to serve its donors' interests. Families are interested in church programs that allow them to spend quality time together.

Upgrade mailings are also a mainstay of church membership programs. Every three years, or more often, members are invited to increase their annual gifts to a higher level. This works for some supporters.

Successful churches invest in member mailing campaigns for the bulk of the annual appeal.

> ### Annual Giving During a Capital Campaign
>
> During my church's capital campaign, a three-year annual gift commitment option was offered as part of its fundraising efforts. We were able to take our annual campaign to a new high. Don't let anyone tell you that annual campaigns and membership decline during capital campaigns.
>
> --Linda

stories from the real world

Telephone campaigns by paid callers or volunteers can be effective methods for acquiring new donors. Churches can track donations by defining gifts as *new*, *renewed*, and *returned*. Returned donors are those who have previously donated but were taken off the membership rolls, and now they are members again.

Churches can track annual giving on a daily, weekly, or monthly basis in order to compare year to year with their own history or with a peer church. In this case, donor numbers can be inflated depending in what day of the month a report is run and when the rolls are purged at around five months *after* the gift comes due.

Churches could also consider having all annual solicitations begin the same day of the year. There could be significant cost savings generated by reducing the number of mailings and constant reminders throughout the year.

Elements of Strong Annual Reporting

Your successful annual campaign drive will culminate in publication of donors' names in an annual report or newsletter. It can also include member names, at least, at higher levels. The report celebrates the success of the annual solicitation, illustrates the impact on the church community, and formally recognizes and thanks donors and volunteers. Think of it as a cultivation opportunity.

Include these elements your annual report/reporting:

◆ An inspiring letter from the church pastor (written by or drafted for the pastor)

◆ One or more personal stories about how the annual campaign is impacting the life of someone in your church community or someone outside your church community, whether it is a student, a member, a staff member, or volunteer

◆ Inspirational stories about major or planned gifts

◆ Statement of revenue and expenditures

◆ Statistics on number of church members served, number of donors, etc. (this can also include giving for missions)

◆ Donors by category

◆ Giving by church leaders and key staff

◆ A letter from the lay leader

◆ Future challenges and goals of the church (plans for the next fundraising campaign)

◆ A response vehicle for those who want to send an extra gift or for those whose names were not listed in this annual report and who want to be included in the next issue

Annual operating dollars may be the most difficult dollars for a church to raise. But it also provides meaningful involvement for new volunteers. It is a tried-and-true method of turning those same volunteers into future prospective church leaders. The annual campaign provides church leaders and financial development committee members with experience in asking for major gifts. It also identifies those who will not make personal solicitations.

The annual campaign strengthens your connections with donors and members. It enables you to communicate opportunities, as well as your successes and needs. It creates a tradition of giving for friends of the church and lays the foundation for capital and endowment gifts. It is a time for identifying, cultivating, and involving new prospects.

To Recap

◆ The annual campaign is likely the most important fundraising effort at your church, providing needed unrestricted dollars—and it comes around *every* year.

◆ It will be important that you and your fundraising team set up and manage the annual campaign carefully. You will need a compelling case for support, trained and enthusiastic volunteer leaders, and a written plan of action for direct mail, telephoning, and personal solicitation of major gifts.

◆ Giving and pledging generates needed unrestricted dollars for your church and gives you assurance your budget will be met beyond what comes in the offering plate.

◆ Faith-based organizations must regularly practice good stewardship including producing an annual report of donors. While that is not the norm for churches, it is something they should consider as they change their culture of giving.

◆ Annual campaign efforts will enhance your ability to raise even larger gifts for capital projects and endowment in the future.

Chapter Eight

Your Major Gifts Strategy is the Fastest Way to Raise More Funds

IN THIS CHAPTER

- ---→ Why people donate money

- ---→ Why is it important to ask for major gift support in person?

- ---→ How to ask

- ---→ How to avoid common mistakes made by inexperienced solicitors

Fundraising is not a talent that comes naturally to most people. Most of us fear rejection. As a church leader, however, you must talk about money—a lot. It helps to see fundraising as part of the larger cause; a means to a greater end. Donor support is a natural outgrowth of commitment.

People support causes they are passionate about. They usually become passionate because they have a personal experience with it. Those who give to the church are no different. They are committed to their faith and demonstrate their gratitude to their church community through financial support.

Perhaps the greatest anxiety-producing part of leading a church fundraising effort is asking people for money. This chapter offers step-by-step instructions for getting in front of the prospective donor and for asking for money. Using our method will reduce your anxiety and allow you to focus on what's important: the donor.

Inexperienced solicitors tend to rush in and make mistakes. Those mistakes often result in money being left on the table, *money that the donor wants to put to good use supporting the ministries of your church.* Read further to discover common mistakes to avoid and increase the funds available for ministry.

It also helps to know the key reasons people donate money:

- ◆ They have money

- ◆ They believe in your cause

◆ They want to impact other people's lives

◆ They trust the solicitor

◆ Their family has a tradition of giving back

But the greatest reason people give money is ... because they are asked!

People give to causes they care about if there is a demonstrated need for their support. The obvious way to show that your church programs and ministries need financial support is to ask for it. However, too often, church leaders do not point out that the support for church programs and ministries is vital. Too often, church leaders *assume* people know this; making such an assumption is what can cripple a church. Those in leadership positions must continually (not just during fundraising time) show that programs and ministries are only possible through their generosity. And then ask for their financial support.

Your first efforts at fundraising can begin with thank-you calls. These are the least-threatening type of personal contacts to make.

A Personal Visit is Powerful!

When I first started my fundraising career, I visited every donor who gave at least $100 to the annual fund. I showed up in person to thank the donor for recent support. Donors appreciated the personal contact so much they sometimes got out their checkbooks and gave me additional gifts—and I didn't even have to ask! A personal visit is very powerful.

At my next job, the number of donors was larger and I couldn't visit every $100 donor, so I visited every $1,000 donor. Again, the amount of the gift doesn't matter. Pick whatever target works for your church. Just make contact and get started!

—Linda

stories from the real world

You may also uncover some pastoral issues. Take this opportunity for what it is and address the issues first. Set aside any fundraising agenda in order to fulfill your pastoral role. If you are a lay leader and uncover issues, ask your donor's permission before turning it over to a clergy person.

The primary goal of a visit to a major donor is to get the next gift. While you might start small until you become more comfortable talking about giving to your church, *your goal as a church leader is to raise major gifts for your church.* While you are visiting with a donor in the donor's office, you can conduct your own research on the expected level of giving and consider the appropriate amount to ask for on the next visit or follow-up.

Statistically, the average time between identification of a major prospect and the receipt of a gift is usually eighteen months. The period in between is for relationship building. This cultivation period allows the prospective donor to get to know you and your church, to understand the mission, to see connections between their values and the church's work, and to gain confidence in the church leadership. Your role in cultivation is to help the prospect fully grasp the importance of the project for which you are raising funds. You want to involve and engage the prospect and treat the congregant like an insider. You will want to practice patience, and begin cultivation well ahead of your campaign.

After the cultivation period, *you will need to ask for a gift in person.* Major gifts rarely arrive unsolicited. Practice a few times before the actual ask. All major gift prospects deserve a strategy that has been vetted with the development team and key volunteers who may know the prospect better than you do. That first time is a little unnerving. But once you have done it and have been successful, each solicitation experience becomes easier. In fact, some church leaders even come to enjoy the process of soliciting major gifts for their beloved church home.

For that reason, select the person or couple for your first ask based on their likelihood of saying *yes*. Choose the low-hanging fruit so that you can get a feel for how a successful visit will go. You will be energized by that success to make your next calls.

Arranging the Meeting

People give to people. Letters, telephone calls, or casual encounters can only go so far. The best solicitations are conducted in person. Few people will refuse a visit if you have emphasized that a topic is too important to merely discuss by phone.

Landing the appointment for the ask is sometimes the hardest part of a solicitation. Making the appointment can be accomplished by a letter with a follow-up call, an email with a follow-up call, an email, or a telephone call. The message to convey is that this visit is so important and exciting to you, that it deserves a face-to-face meeting.

You also need to consider who else, if anyone, should accompany you on the visit. Two solicitors can be better than one. Having a board member or staff member accompany you on a visit can make the importance of the visit more evident. It can also give you greater confidence. Consider taking the staff person who manages the program that most interests your prospective giver. The most people either of us has ever taken on a visit was five, and we got the result we wanted!

An appointment can take place in an office or home or at a restaurant over breakfast or lunch. Of course, you can invite prospects to the church, but the prospect's home turf is ideal. Once the appointment is made, confirm it in writing.

> ## How Many People Should You Take on the Appointment?
>
> Two solicitors are usually better than one.
>
> **observation**

If you or others are making a call together, plan to meet before your appointment. You must decide who takes which parts of the conversation. You should also agree on who is responsible for providing any follow-up materials or information. Establishing each person's primary roles ahead of time will reduce any anxiety that may arise.

The Ask

When you arrive at the meeting, take a few moments to establish rapport. Look around the person's office and ask about photos or awards, or discuss a common point of interest, such as their affiliation with the church as a volunteer, member, or board member. If the prospect is a parent, make sure you know how their kids are doing and if they have interest in the church and whether there are any superlatives to mention.

Share news of the church, perhaps a recent event or recognition of members, in a local publication. Try to share something that the person may not have heard any other way, or that is news that is not yet published anywhere. Then, after you have made general comments, get to the point of your visit. "Would you consider supporting [name of project] at our church?"

In making the ask, your demeanor is more important than following an exact script. You must be passionate, you must express the importance of the gift, you must demonstrate your understanding of the prospect, and you must convey your confidence in the success of the campaign. Also, make sure that you have already made your own gift to the cause.

When you make the request, ask for a specific amount. Your preparation in advance of the call should have given you an indication of the prospect's capability, level of giving to similar projects, and level of interest in your church. Aim high. We can think of no time in our careers that a prospective donor was insulted by being asked for too much. In a few cases, the donor gave even more than what was asked.

If appropriate, share the amount of your own stretch gift. Mention that all church leaders and good friends of the church are being asked to participate at a leadership level. Point out recognition that will be available. For some prospects, naming recognition will make a difference in the amount of their gift.

> ### The Importance of Recognition
>
> I once had someone contact my office and all she said was, "What do you get for $1 million?" I responded with three options, none of which interested the donor. Finally, I described the best naming option we had available from the recent capital campaign.
>
> When the donor asked, "How much is that?" I said with trepidation, "$3 million." She replied, "I'll take that one."
>
> —Linda

stories from the real world

Never Underestimate the Importance of Recognition

Some prospects will want recognition for their gifts. Some prefer to remain anonymous. You should be prepared either way with a list of options with giving levels clearly marked. Once donors sign pledge cards or letters of intent, you will need to clarify the donor's wishes regarding the recognition options.

Look the prospect in the eye and ask these three magic words, "Would you consider a gift of xxx for our yyy project?"

Then pause. Keep your silence and *let them be the next to speak.*

Some novice solicitors jump in too quickly here. Resist the temptation to do so. Give the prospect time to think about what you are asking and time to respond. Remember, this is a suggestion, not a demand. It sets expectations and is a starting point for further discussion. You are telling the prospective donor how to make a difference and how to fit into your campaign or project.

Anticipating the Prospect's Response

There are four possible outcomes to your solicitation:

◆   Hopefully, the prospective donor will say yes, at which time you thank the donor, confirm the details, leave, and follow up immediately with a personal letter of appreciation.

◆   The prospective donor may say no. You will need to actively listen to the rationale given. Restate the concern. Is it no to the project? No to the amount? No to the timing? No never? Probing may lead to a negotiation. No may actually mean *not now.*

◆   Another outcome is, "I will think about it." You will need to probe a bit to see if you can provide additional details for consideration. And schedule a time to get back with the prospect. If you have met with one-half of a couple, they may need to confer before deciding. Affirm that plan of action.

◆   The fourth possible outcome is that there may be some objection. Be prepared to answer all questions about the project. If you don't know the answer, say so, and use this as an opportunity to return and provide more details. The prospect's personal circumstances will sometimes preclude a gift.

It is always helpful to have anticipated possible objections in advance and to have strategized your answers. This can be discussed and rehearsed with staff and/or volunteers before the visit. Listen actively. Pause before responding. Restate what you hear. Ask open-ended questions. Summarize the positives and look for areas of agreement, acceptance, and interest.

Follow-up Actions

Compare notes and results with the development officer and other volunteers who are making similar calls. Make sure all solicitors are providing strong, consistent information about your church.

Bring a letter of intent or pledge form with you on the visit. It can be provided to the prospect and completed on the spot, or used as a leave-behind. At any rate, you will need to follow up to receive the final commitment. In many cases, a written pledge to pay before the end of the fiscal year will suffice. When you are raising money for a special project, your donor may be able to make a larger gift if it can be paid over several years. You must decide ahead of time if that is acceptable to your project.

> ### What Exactly Are They Supporting?
>
> *Asking people for money is giving them the opportunity to put their resources at the disposal of the Kingdom.*
>
> —Henri J.M. Nouwen
>
> **" "**

If you did not obtain a firm commitment on the visit, follow up with a phone call in a few days and stay in touch until the pledge/gift is confirmed in writing. A verbal pledge should be confirmed with a letter (including a return envelope) sent in the next few days specifying the payment details. It is usually best for the original solicitor to be the person to follow up to complete the gift in the days following the solicitation.

If the solicitation is successful, you should ask the prospect two questions:

◆ Are there others who might be interested in the project?

◆ How would you like to be involved in the project going forward? (You would be surprised how often prospects warm up to the idea and then involve themselves in the campaign.)

Recording details of the visit in person or by phone, mail, or email will help the development team plan for recognition activities and for future projects. If the answer was no, any concerns can be addressed and the prospect can be solicited again when/if those concerns have been alleviated.

Avoid These Common Mistakes

As a church leader, you should be optimistic and enthusiastic and persistent. Don't fall victim to the most common pitfalls of soliciting:

◆ Soliciting others without making your own gift first

◆ Not asking for a specific amount

◆ Not asking in person

◆ Not providing appropriate follow-up

Practice Makes Perfect

During church campaigns, we typically hold solicitation practice sessions with the church pastor, the campaign chair, and others the day before a major gift call. We cover who would say what and when. Our merry bands become so effective that we rehearse in the car on the way to meet the prospective donor. And by the end of the campaign, we so improve in our delivery that we can cover each other's roles.

Comfortable relationships among solicitors and donors will be helpful in moving donors from major gifts to ultimate gifts for your church.

To Recap

◆   The greatest reason people give money is because they are asked.

◆   It takes practice to ask for a gift comfortably.

◆   You will want to do your homework.

◆   Perhaps take someone else along with you who knows the prospect, too.

◆   It may take eighteen months to complete a major gift.

Chapter Nine

Capital Campaigns Will Likely Occur During Your Tenure. Be Prepared!

IN THIS CHAPTER

- ---➔ Create a case for support for your capital needs

- ---➔ Identify and solicit the top ten gifts first

- ---➔ The capital campaign process just keeps on going, usually in three- to five-year cycles

Most churches are either in a capital campaign, getting ready for a campaign, or finishing a campaign. In this chapter, we will review precampaign planning, getting organized, and the role of the church board/leadership, followed by the details of an active campaign and the importance of stewardship.

Campaign activities usually stretch out over a five-year period. The first year or two include precampaign planning activities: Does your church have an updated strategic plan? Is there a business plan that follows the strategy? Have you educated and cultivated your constituencies? Have your plans been costed out with an architect and/or engineer? Have you conducted an internal and external readiness assessment? Have you evaluated your case for support and do you have a written campaign plan?

The active campaign begins a year or two later with a board solicitation, followed by solicitation of your top donors and prospects. Always solicit the best prospects first, followed by the next best prospects. A public phase comes at the end of the campaign when most of the money has been raised.

Years three to five are for stewarding donors. You must do what you promised you would do when you presented them with your case for support. Collect the pledges and communicate campaign results.

Campaigns begin with a solid base of support. Your board and you as church leader will provide the vision and mission of a campaign. It should be clearly articulated in a written strategic and business plan. How familiar are you with the fundraising history of your church? Do you have donors and prospects with the capacity and propensity to give? Prospect identification and research should include your own church

Capital Campaign Timeline

Precampaign - 1-2 Years	Active Campaign - 1-3 Years	Stewardship - 3-5 Years
Strategic Plan	Board Solicitation	Do What Was Promised
Business Plan	Top 10 Gifts	Collect Pledges
Education	Lead Gifts	Named-gift Recognition
Cultivation	Major Gifts	Communications
Costing	Public Campaign	
Internal Readiness	Victory Celebrations	
External Readiness		
Revise/Refine		
Campain Plan		

congregation's giving history, a simple Google search of individuals to augment giving information beyond your church records, and wealth screening of your entire database by a reputed firm.

The ministerial/administrative staff should be well trained and familiar with constituents. You must have an accurate database, and information must be readily available for staff and volunteer solicitors. Hopefully, years of successful annual campaign solicitations have prepared you for this step.

Your church leadership and senior staff must participate in the campaign at a leadership level. There should be openness about the financial health and track record of the church. Information will need to be confidentially shared with individuals involved in the campaign.

What are the long-term needs of your church? What's your ideal church size? What buildings need to be added or renovated in the next five to ten years? What are the corresponding costs? What will be desired outcomes of these expenditures? Is there a commitment to the process and to the proposed budget?

What is the specific project plan? Usually there are more needs than funding permits, so priorities must be set. What is the rationale or case for support of the priorities? What is the exact cost of each item in the plan? Is there a benefit to the donors/prospects as well as to the church? What is the projected timeline? What will be the end results of a campaign?

The campaign planning committee provides staff and volunteer leadership. It is usually comprised of three to eight people. The committee oversees the case development, and the study process.

Role of Fundraising Counsel

We are often asked about the role of counsel during a campaign. Counsel can help guide each stage of the process, identify red flags, and help you avoid costly detours. Counsel offers objectivity and experience. Counsel can also provide training for staff and volunteers. Sometimes, your leadership may just need to hear feedback from an outside source. Counsel can be most useful if your development team or key volunteers have never participated in a campaign before.

 practical tip

Capital Campaigns—The Origin Story

Take notice in the flow of the solicitation phase of campaign activities. Be aware of the critical path of activities:

◆ Identify the need.

◆ Communicate the need.

◆ Get the commitment of the leadership.

◆ Those leaders invite those they lead to join in.

◆ Direct that group to engage the next level of leaders.

◆ Continue down the pipeline until all have had an opportunity to contribute.

◆ Achieve success.

◆ Celebrate that success.

This critical path is so significant that it has been around a long time. For several thousands of years, in fact. We find this model for raising capital funding back in the Old Testament. Go grab your Bible (or Bible app on your smart phone) and check out 1 Chronicles 29.

Right now, pause your reading of this chapter, and look up this important passage. Read it and then come back to this section. We'll wait right here.

You just read that when it came time for the temple to be built (the need was identified) David and Solomon set about a logical, progressive plan to raise what was needed. First, as the head of the assembly should do, David gave of his own resources. Then he asked his inner circle—the leaders of the tribes—to join him in offerings to build this house for the Lord. Next, those in the inner circle turned to their leaders and commanders and invited them to give as they were able. And so forth until all were included. Each, in turn, committed themselves and their treasure to the Lord, and to the building of the temple.

Some gave gold for the things of gold. Some gave silver for the things of silver. And bronze and stones and of their various types of treasure. Gifts in kind were the basis for the building of the temple. Each gave as they could and it took all of them—from leaders down to those who were led, and from all the tribes—to achieve success. And they had an abundance of offerings with which to build the temple.

Then David blessed all that was given and praised God for enabling the generosity that had poured forth.

Finally, notice what they did at the end: They came together, they shared a meal, and they thanked and praised God together. That's the way to successfully complete your capital campaign—join together, take the journey along the critical path, and celebrate what God can do with a community of faithful people!

!
important

Committee members will also be asked to help identify and cultivate donors and help recruit the campaign leadership.

An internal assessment identifies the resources needed to run a campaign. What would be needed in terms of staffing and other support to overlay a campaign on an already functioning stewardship operation? Several steps occur before a campaign is initiated.

Prior to committing to a campaign, a third party typically conducts a feasibility study, especially if the amount to be raised is a significant amount above any annual fundraising. The study is based on objective, personal interviews with potential donors, leaders, and church influencers. A pave-the-way letter is sent to interviewees. Appointments are set, interviews are conducted.

Outside counselors can be good listeners and strategists. They can often elicit information that interviewees are hesitant to share with the church leadership.

The case study helps fine-tune the campaign plan and case for support. It floats a preliminary goal and proposes a range of gifts. It should also identify the top ten gifts and the important next steps in campaign leadership and strategies for recruitment. Analysis and recommendations are provided in a final report and plan of action.

A feasibility study usually takes three to six months, but timing depends on the development of the case and the availability of interviewees. The cost of a study depends on the number of interviews conducted and the geographical location of interviewees.

How do you know when you are ready for a campaign? Do you know what the needs are for your church? Are costs firmly established? Does the staff and lay leadership agree with and understand the campaign process? How will the campaign impact the annual budget and the church community it serves? Are there adequate staff and resources to operate a campaign? Is your donor community willing to support a campaign? If so, at what level of support and when?

Creating Campaign Communications

The goal of campaign communications is to induce action. Who are your donors and what are their motivations for giving? The number one reason for giving is to help others. In churches, people give to campaigns because they believe in your church's mission and goals and it is an opportune time in their lives. If asked appropriately, they will contribute.

Your connection with prospects must be highly personal. Campaign writing is not like other writing. Campaign communications must persuade, show empathy, and then induce action. Make the case for support long enough to explain why dollars are needed, but short enough to keep their attention.

Tell donor stories, show how giving has helped, and feature campaign leadership saying why they serve on the campaign committee. Let the church's character shine through. Campaign objectives must be clear, simple, and compelling.

As a first step, develop an outline or script. Write the narrative in bullets. Use quotes and examples. Invest in great visual aids. A picture is worth a thousand words.

Don't use jargon, insider acronyms, or empty words. Say what makes your church distinctive; don't use language that could represent just any church. Use verbs. Invest in writers and designers, whether in-house or contract. A professional-looking case statement can make a profound difference in the campaign.

Engage your reader with examples and stories. Be clear about expected action. Say it plainly. Visualize and summarize. Let someone else read/review the final draft. Ask for feedback.

Your church should be up front and honest in the case. How would you describe your institution? What are the church's strengths and distinctions? Who benefits from your work, in your church, in your local community, and in the larger world?

Describe the campaign. What is the goal and purpose? Is it a comprehensive campaign? Is there a capital, endowment, or annual operating component? Will the campaign be phased? How will this campaign move your institution forward? Be sure to create a picture of what happens if donors do not give.

Campaign Materials

Campaigns benefit from professional-looking case statements which tell donor stories.

important

Why is the capital project necessary? Will more people in your church circle be served? Better served? Will systems be more efficient? Is the need due to growth in membership? What are the costs of each component or phase? How much is in hand? Will there be financing?

How will this campaign affect the people you serve? How is this campaign an opportunity for your donor to make this happen? How can your donors be assured that this is a wise investment?

Define gift-naming opportunities. These can include buildings, rooms, a donor wall, founding donors, time-limited named spaces, named endowment funds, or expendable named program funds.

Churches should consider time-limited spaces. Ten to fifteen years is a suggested length of time. The purpose of the space may change over time and even if it doesn't, renovation will likely be required. The original donors can be given first right of refusal and be invited to provide funds to maintain the space beyond the original ten to fifteen years.

There should be transparency and trust between donors and the church. Share cost estimates and what they are based on. Summarize the way the church manages and invests funds. Establish or review endowed-gift guidelines and spending policies. Show a summary of the operating budget and business plan impact.

Named Spaces

I always keep at the tip of my fingers a list of named spaces at my institution. I always keep a list of approved naming opportunities as well.

You see, a one-time guest in our church came to me looking for Great Aunt Susie's named room. None of us on the current staff knew or remembered Great Aunt Susie or where her room was. Since then, I have never missed an opportunity to share with guests whatever information they desire. I also made sure to provide the list of named spaces to all departments that might receive guests at our church. We should all know where Great Aunt Susie's space is.

—Linda

stories from the real world

Making a Strong Case

When making your case, keep these in mind:

◆ The case statement is designed to support solicitations.

◆ A sound case provides the rationale for raising money.

◆ All solicitors should be able to summarize the case in their own words in less than ten minutes.

Campaign materials should include a letter from the campaign chair, leadership lists, titles, relationship to the church; architect's renderings/floor plans/models; site or master plans; statements of endorsement, frequently asked questions; examples and stories.

Provide a list of any and all ways to give. What methods of payment will be accepted? Is there a specific time period (i.e., three- to five-year pledges)? What types of gifts are accepted? Will planned gifts count in the campaign? What types of gifts will be recognized in the campaign? Where should gifts be sent? Who should be contacted for questions about the campaign?

Most donors expect churches to manage campaign costs effectively. Know the quantity of materials you will need in advance or you can print on demand.

Proposals, letters of intent, and personalized updates, including named-gift opportunities, are all part of the campaign production package.

Other campaign pieces include pledge forms, folders, stationery, envelopes, matching invitations, and newsletters. Electronic versions can be shown on a DVD, on an iPad, on smartphones, through email, or on the website.

Campaign Leadership

Church members and ministerial staff play many roles in a campaign. Each can be the visionary, leader, advocate, donor, cultivator, solicitor, and steward. Campaign committee members must play a leadership role in all phases of the campaign. One hundred percent participation of the campaign committee and church leadership early in the campaign is essential. Giving at a leadership level is also expected. The committee must approve the campaign plan. All committee members should help solicit gifts.

A main function of individual volunteer committees is to bring potential donors to you. A main function of the staff stewardship office is to organize these meetings.

The campaign committee should be made up of leadership-level donors. They should be knowledgeable about fundraising practices and meet regularly to approve policies, plans, and strategies. It is acceptable to have members on the committee who are not yet on the church leadership team or board.

Campaign committee members should cultivate, solicit, and steward gifts. They should be part of evaluating the fundraising successes and challenges and be truly involved in the campaign.

Church Leadership Solicitation First

The church leadership solicitation is the first step in the campaign itself. The church leadership solicitation plan includes recruitment strategies for the campaign chairs, evaluation of capacity and inclination of each proposed committee member, determination of the ask amount, and setting of a preliminary dollar goal. The church leadership participation goal should always be 100 percent. Is a challenge gift possible? Campaign committee members should be solicited in person by their peers.

The stewardship committee can approve or serve as the campaign study committee. It can retain counsel. It can educate the other church leaders about their role as lead donors and solicitors. It can also serve as the campaign committee after the study is completed.

A precious commodity church leaders provide is in leadership recruitment. Campaign committee members should be major donors, provide access to donors, and be willing to visit and ask. They should understand and support the campaign plan.

The leadership organization can be defined by group: the board, the staff, and any additional board advisory groups. They can also be defined by size of gift: lead, major, general, or public.

Initial Campaign Organization

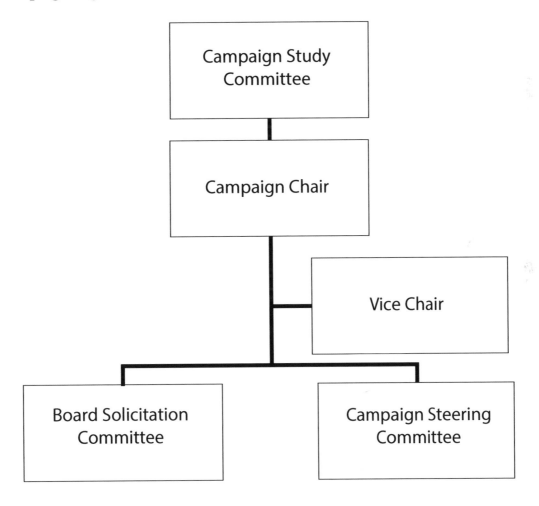

The leadership groups in the campaign can be organized sequentially over time. There should be one volunteer for every five prospects. The best volunteers should solicit the bigger prospects.

Honorary chairs are not usually necessary. Campaign committees must have report meetings. A campaign leader needs to be a significant donor. Political leadership does not equal philanthropic leadership.

Campaign committee members should have written job descriptions with clear expectations. Volunteers should be recruited in person by someone difficult to refuse. Board leadership and the ministerial team are critical to campaign success.

Three Secrets

As with all fundraising, the three secrets to fundraising success in a capital campaign are:

◆   A compelling case for support.

◆   Strong leadership.

◆   A written strategy/plan.

Leadership is the most important of the three secrets to campaign fundraising success.

important

A written plan requires self-discipline. The minister and staff must understand and buy in to the campaign plan. Then there must be volunteer involvement in approving and implementing the plan. Writing the plan down identifies weaknesses and challenges of the campaign components. The plan also specifies who does what, when, where, why, and how.

It is as important to know what *not* to do as it is to know what *to* do. Some church leaders have a desire for publicity. There is an urge to solicit broad-based support too soon. Campaigns should not have publicity and broad-based support until the final stage of a campaign. There is also the phenomenon of having too few meetings and *new* plans and that *our campaign is unique.*

An essential campaign strategy builds momentum. There is a range-of-gifts chart, a schedule or calendar and, of course, lists of prospects. Campaign momentum can be built with a challenge gift, the church leader campaign, leadership recruitment, and/or a staff campaign.

In developing a range-of-gifts table, the top gift needed is usually about 20 percent of the total goal. The top ten to thirty gifts usually make up about one-half of the campaign total. Public or general membership gifts are 10 percent or less of the total.

A range-of-gifts table educates the campaign leadership about expected gift size. It informs prospective donors. It focuses all campaign workers on the top ten gifts.

An essential strategy element of the campaign is the schedule. There can be as many as five phases: the campaign preparation, the top ten gifts, other leadership gifts, major gifts, and the public phase.

The top ten gifts average up to 50 percent of the total campaign goal. The second tier of the range of gifts is the lead-gift level. Major gifts are also all personal solicitations. The public phase is when you bring visibility to the campaign and the total is usually less than 10 percent of the campaign goal. The larger the campaign, the longer the top-gift phase and the higher the dollar value of the amount to be raised. People who make large gifts generally do not make quick decisions. There will likely need to be a period of cultivation before the actual ask and before the gift decision.

The campaign committee should personally solicit gifts and provide insight for solicitation strategies as well as motivate other volunteers and campaign leadership. Staff should handle the rest of the details. The stewardship office should prepare written talking points, solicitation materials, and proposals. It should also draft all correspondence, coordinate meetings, and handle solicitation tracking.

An action-item report should include the prospect name, the projected ask amount, the assigned solicitor and staff back up, the last action date, and the next step and date.

The campaign will continue to move forward if the campaign committee practices intentional contacts, cultivation, solicitation, and closing. When one action closes, another opens. The committee should meet regularly and use email and voicemail as tools in between.

$10 Million Range-of-Gifts Table

No. of Gifts	Size ($)	Total ($)	Cumulative ($)	Percent (%)
1	2,000,000	2,000,000	2,000,000	20
1	1,000,000	1,000,000	3,000,000	30
3	500,000	1,500,000	4,500,000	45
5	250,000	1,250,000	5,750,000	57
10	100,000	1,000,000	6,750,000	67
20	50,000	1,000,000	7,750,000	77
40	25,000	1,000,000	8,750,000	87
60	10,000	600,000	9,350,000	93
Many	<10,000	650,000	10,000,000	100%

Example

The Annual Campaign During a Capital Campaign

Every church will need to decide how to integrate or separate annual fund/membership/operating campaigns and capital campaign priorities. Joint asks for major donors and prospects are often used. It is possible to grow the annual campaign and membership during a capital campaign by using multiyear pledges, challenge grants, and recognition in giving societies. Social media is most useful to a campaign during the public phase and annual giving fundraising activities.

Stewardship

Donor cultivation and acknowledgment/stewardship is not only important to the current campaign but to future campaigns as well. There should be an official confirmation letter within twenty-four hours of a campaign gift commitment. If a signed letter of intent has not been received, this is the grateful and specific request for the letter of intent.

During the next few days, an additional acknowledgment should come from the campaign chair. Other leadership, including the solicitor, should follow up with the prospect to receive the final signed letter of intent.

Pledge reminders should be sent at appropriate times throughout the campaign. Window envelopes or something that looks like an invoice should be avoided. Form letters should not replace relationships and relationship building. Personalized pledge reminders, with telephone calls, are another cultivation opportunity. Each pledge payment should be treated as a new gift.

Victory

It is important to officially end the campaign. It is always nice to hold a victory celebration for all of the volunteers. Host a victory celebration for all staff. Write donors to let them know that the campaign goal has been reached. Seek ways to keep volunteers/ donors involved in new activities. Provide any and all donor-recognition signage that was promised. Be creative and sincere.

Preparation for the next campaign should begin immediately. The campaign plan should be evaluated and updated. Final financial and donor reports should be prepared. Provide cash flow reports that detail pledge payments. Review all open pledges and any necessary write-offs. Analyze refusals and any prospects that did not yet make commitments. Follow up on any outstanding gift opportunities. Make recommendations for improvements in the next campaign while campaign activities are fresh in mind.

Things to Watch Out for in a Campaign

Just as we gave you a list of items vital to a successful campaign, there are items that are critical to avoid. Taking shortcuts or doing what seems easiest will get you to the finish line faster, but it won't raise the money you need for your ministries. If you fall prey to the easy route and avoid the necessary work, you will certainly leave money on the table.

- ◆ Prematurely announcing the public campaign

- ◆ Lack of leadership

- ◆ No committee meetings/structure

- ◆ Not asking for specific amounts

- ◆ Not asking in person

- ◆ Too much dependence on one donor

- ◆ Lack of follow-through to close gifts

Characteristics of a Successful Campaign

We have guided many churches through various fundraising campaigns. Because of that, we have identified the vital elements needed in a campaign to be successful. Note that this list is not to be accomplished in order; rather, most items are to be approached simultaneously.

- ❏ Understand the top ten gifts

- ❏ Sequential fundraising

- ❏ Personal solicitations

- ❏ Specific ask amounts

- ❏ 100 percent board/leadership support

- ❏ Church director involvement

- ❏ Trained, experienced staff

- ❏ Budget as an expense 3 to 5 percent of the amount to be raised

- ❏ Counsel

To Recap

- ◆ Most churches are in some form of campaign—beginning one, implementing one, or ending one.

- ◆ With good planning, the campaign process can take up to five years, including cultivation and stewardship/acknowledgment.

- ◆ The top ten gifts received in a campaign can provide invaluable information as to the potential of the total amount that can be raised and show exactly where the church leaders' time should be spent.

- ◆ With determination and consistent follow through, churches can effectively raise funds for their much needed capital improvements.

Chapter Ten

Endowment Building is Critical for the Future of Your Church

IN THIS CHAPTER

···→ Endowment is critical to your church's long-term financial success

···→ Build an endowment

···→ Initiate a planned giving program and educate all of your constituents

E ndowment is critical to the future of churches. How large an endowment should your church have? This chapter focuses on how to create and build an endowment for your church through planned giving and education of your constituency groups.

What is the size of your church endowment? Some say—and we agree—the optimum size for a church endowment is three to five times your annual budget. You can do the math.

Why have an endowment? How do we start one? What is an acceptable spending rule? Should we have different funds in our endowment? What is meant by a quasi-endowment? What is the market value of your endowment? How many endowment funds do you have, if any?

What is the amount of income from your endowment funds generated for your annual operating budget? These financial questions are important to the future planning for churches.

You know you are ready for endowment building when you have defined your mission and you have a solid financial base, a growing donor pool, and the highest-quality product for donors to invest in. As with any other type of campaign, the church leadership needs to be committed to endowment for fundraising to be successful. It helps to have a long-term history of annual giving to allow you to profile and prospect among annual donors. And there always needs to be a balance between asking for operating, endowment, and capital needs.

Creating a Planned Giving Program

Planned gifts are generally defined as charitable gift instruments that transfer assets to the church for current use, including bequests in wills, charitable gift annuities, charitable trusts, life insurance policies, real estate, and split-interest gifts. These gift arrangements often have special tax benefits to the donor, and allow gifts of accumulated assets at the end of the donor's life or at a time most beneficial to the donor. The good news is you don't have to be an expert in planned giving to begin a planned giving program at your organization.

The church will need to set up an endowment account with a local bank or firm. The church leadership will need to be committed to building a stream of secure, continued earnings from the endowment to provide predictable dollar support for the annual operating budget. The investment of the endowment funds must ensure continuing income support of operations. Leadership will need to manage the risk and set financial targets.

Most churches will be starting from zero on an endowment. Providing structure to get your church's endowment off the ground will be helpful. Three possible committees that can have separate duties will keep them focused:

> **Building an Endowment Through Planned Giving**
>
> The best way to create or build an endowment is through planned giving. Eighty percent of planned gifts are made through bequests.
>
> Bequests represent language in a will leaving a simple percentage or dollar amount to a relative or charity. This provides tax benefits to the dying person's estate and benefits the recipient. All of us should have a will.
>
> **principle**

◆ A legacy society committee should identify, cultivate, ask, and steward donors.

◆ An investment committee would increase the endowment through careful investment of funds, monitoring interest rates, and adjusting spending rules as needed.

◆ A grants committee decides how to spend the funds, if the funds are undesignated. Grants may be made with a certain percentage going to programs or maintenance or where the need is greatest.

These three committees should have cross committee membership, so that one hand knows what the other is doing.

Most churches set a goal of 5 percent return over the long term. Some churches use a five-year rolling average to calculate spending. To calculate this average, add up the fair market value of the fund (FMV) on a certain date for each of the last five years. Divide by five to get the average FMV over those five years. Then multiply the percentage you spend of that average FMV. This averages the value of the fund so that you do not spend a lot in a year the fund has high market value, then not so much in a bad-earnings year. Spending averages out as the market fluctuates.

Church leaders need to engage an endowment investment manager working in conjunction with the finance and/or investment committees of the church (along with the church CFO/treasurer or bookkeeper) to manage the funds, enforce the policies, and monitor spending.

The first step to creating a planned giving program is to craft a compelling case for endowment, conveying a sense of urgency and explaining the impact of endowment growth. You must engage leadership and then draft an endowment plan or strategy.

How many planned giving commitments does your church have already?

Who are your best prospects? What is the best strategy for your church?

Someone will need to do some homework first. This is likely the development officer or whoever is on the staff that is responsible for chairing the annual pledge drive/fundraising. Some churches hire planned giving/major gifts officers. If you do hire a person dedicated to planned giving at your church, it will be important not to have too high of expectations in the beginning. Many churches have had start-and-stop programs because there were no realized planned gifts in the first years. Planned giving is a long-term solution to your church's future funding. There must be clear expectations among your church leaders before initiating a planned giving program.

What is the total of realized bequests your church has received to date? Has this number of bequests been tracked over time? What is the average bequest gift that has been received?

What is the total of lifetime gifts that have come to your church from bequest donors? What is the ratio of bequest gifts to lifetime gifts for your donors? What is the percentage of bequest donors who were annual fund donors? This information can give you insights for what you might expect from similar donors and prospects.

You must establish clear guidelines to create new permanent funds. What is the fund's purpose? What is the desired size of the endowment fund for your church? What are the naming opportunities? Your business officer working in conjunction with development and your church attorney and CPA can provide appropriate accounting and legal records. There should be a standard document to create an endowment fund and an endowment-acceptance process.

> **Read the Files!**
>
> I have found several planned gift prospects just by reading institutional paper files and talking to long-time church staff members. I was working with a faith-based organization for our denomination when I learned that one of our church members had made a seven-figure bequest to our church. We needed $100,000 to complete our capital campaign, so I coached our pastor and another volunteer on how to ask. They visited the donor and were successful in receiving an immediate gift that completed the campaign—and we still received the full bequest several years later!
>
> —Linda
>
>  stories from the real world

Your church will need to manage active planned giving stewardship that mirrors the stewardship of annual and capital donors. There should be endowment coverage in a church written annual report; annual personal contact with the donor, which can include an annual call from a staff person; an annual handwritten thank-you note; a report on the church overall endowment; a planned giving newsletter; and invitations to events at the church. Each planned giving donor should be assigned to a staff person and tracked in the data system.

Staff Turnover Hurts Fundraising

Turnover in development staff/planned giving committee leadership sometimes causes planned gifts to become *lost* over time. Creating and following through with a three- or five-year plan of stewardship to keep in touch with those who have included the church in their estate plans will make sure the donors know how important they are. While changes in leadership are inevitable, having a lasting plan of action will mitigate the shifting personnel.

Planned Giving Communications

Planned giving should be included as a giving option on the church website. Because of the technical nature of planned giving information, it will be worthwhile to consider expanding your website with more detailed information by using a third-party vendor. There are a number of firms that provide this type of service. A click on a link takes the web viewer from your church site to an expert's planned giving data on another site. There the viewer can calculate giving amounts and find information specific to the donor's situation. Up-to-date tax law information, gift calculators, retirement calculators, and college calculators are all useful tools provided to engage the prospect in the planning process. Most church development officers are not equipped to handle this much detail.

Your church can insert planned giving information into your other development communications: annual report/report at the annual meeting, quarterly or monthly magazine, website, endowment brochure/materials, or planned giving newsletter.

Endowment communications should use clear messages. They should challenge the reader to action. These donors and prospects will merit personal attention. An example of an initial planned giving activity might be to send a special request letter to donors age fifty plus who have given to your church the past five years in a row.

Coordinate with Financial Advisors

All planned giving prospects should be encouraged to consult their own financial and legal advisors before completing a planned gift with your church. Doing so will ensure that the gift plan is structured to meet the donor's best interest, while keeping the role of the church only as a recipient.

principle

A successful planned giving program depends on identifying those elusive planned giving prospects, conducting thorough research, and effectively cultivating them before making the ask.

Consider Three Groups in your Planned Giving Program

By identifying people in each of these categories, you will have a solid list of prospects. Be sure to cultivate the types of prospects according to the method used to identify them. For example, you should approach directly those who are ready to be asked, but be sure to spend time educating those who lack an established relationship with the church.

◆ Those ready to receive an ask

◆ Those that meet the criteria, but where there is not yet an established relationship with the church leadership

◆ Those with an interest in the church

Planned Giving Prospects

A list of planned giving prospects for your church may include people who:

◆ Are well off

◆ Are concerned with the receipt of current income

◆ May want your church to exercise management skills over their assets as they grow older

◆ Are unmarried or widowed

◆ Are married but without children

- Have tax concerns

- Are significant current donors or past donors to your church

- Are getting along in years

- Have some sort of programmatic tie to your church

The Best Planned Giving Prospects

These are the important signals to watch for with your own *best* planned giving prospects:

- Donors who have given five or more years to your church

- Past endowment donors

- Current and past church leaders

- Long-term friends, volunteers, and staff

- Multigenerational families

Select the top ten or twenty or even one hundred prospects that meet more than one of the above criteria to focus on in your church's planned giving program.

Women as Planned Gift Prospects

Don't forget women as potential prospects for all types of gifts to your church. Just as planned giving is the fastest-growing area of philanthropy today, women are the fastest-growing donor population. Statistically, they will outlive their spouses. Women are more likely to make final dispersion of a family's assets.

Educating Donors about Planned Giving

People make planned gifts because they believe in your church and are asked to make a planned gift after being properly educated and cultivated. They know you and one or more of your volunteers and staff. They may need tax advantages. The gift may help the donor save money and, therefore, the donor can pass on more to heirs. This satisfies the donor's personal obligations and charitable interests at the same time. The planned gift places the investment management responsibilities on others (often a trust company, a bank's trust department or, if properly equipped to fulfill trustee duties, the church), an important matter for some older individuals. Assets can then be managed after death for the benefit of the surviving spouse who may be less knowledgeable about financial matters.

While the minister does not need to be an expert in planned giving, clergy and lay leaders must be trained on planned giving messages. You should develop speed-dial relationships with your church attorney and local wealth managers. Some denominations have national or regional associations that may have resources that can help your church in planned giving.

> **Planned Gift Commitments**
>
> People make planned gifts because they believe in your church mission and values and are asked to make a planned gift after being properly educated and cultivated.
>
> **observation**

Your church can and should host seminars on estate planning. These can be for current members, volunteers, and others in the larger community.

Recruit an advisory board of professionals in the community. Educate them about your church and your constituents.

Establish a planned giving recognition or Legacy Society. Plan annual activities for this group to keep them and their families involved in the work of your church.

You and your church can then solicit planned gifts with confidence.

To Recap

◆ Endowment building comes after successful annual and capital fundraising efforts.

◆ Planned giving is the best way to build an endowment.

◆ There are a few simple steps you can take to begin a planned giving program.

◆ You can begin planned giving without breaking your budget.

Chapter Eleven

Innovations in Faith-based Giving

IN THIS CHAPTER

--→ Use electronic giving to encourage consistent giving

--→ Teach your children the importance of sharing resources

--→ By broadening your church's definition of stewardship, you encourage members of your congregation to grow spiritually

Innovations, especially through technology, can jump-start your fundraising in churches as well as faith-based camps and schools. The members of your congregation experience over three thousand messages a day telling them how to spend their time and their money. How often and in what ways do you communicate what your church has to offer them? Once your initial commitment program strategy is laid out, consider what else you should add to the plan to capture the attention of your members, and to keep it relevant.

Why embrace the new? There are many practical and technical innovations that make giving to your church more convenient to your church members. Adapting to these innovations in giving trends will ensure that your revenue stream continues uninterrupted.

More and more, people are leaving their checkbooks at home, and people just don't carry around large amounts of cash so it can be easily placed in your collection basket. Embracing various methods of electronic giving means more revenue through more consistent giving from your congregants. Not only should you intentionally move your members toward electronic giving, it is quickly becoming a best practice of thriving churches who want to encourage giving among more baby boomers, millennials, and younger members.

Popularity of Online Giving

In 2002, only 4 percent of giving was done online—across all sectors, both secular and religious. Ten years later, 65 percent of all giving was done online. At this writing, the numbers point to more than 75 percent.

Transition to Electronic Giving

Giving to all organizations by mailing in a check or by making a phone call is dwindling. While you may offer those who attend worship services a more direct and personal way to give—by placing money directly into the collection plate—chances are, the amount you collect each week is also dwindling. People just don't carry as much cash as they used to, and even fewer people carry around their checkbook.

Funny Money

A well-worn one-dollar bill and a twenty-dollar bill arrived at a Federal Reserve Bank to be retired. As they moved along the conveyor belt, they began a conversation. The twenty-dollar bill reminisced about its travels all over the county.

"I've had a pretty good life," the twenty proclaimed. "Why, I've been to Las Vegas and Atlantic City, the finest restaurants in New York, performances on Broadway, and even a cruise to the Caribbean."

"Wow!" said the one-dollar bill. "You've really had an exciting life!"

"So, tell me," says the twenty, "where have *you* been throughout your lifetime?"

The one-dollar bill replied, "Oh, I've been to the Methodist Church, the Baptist Church, the Lutheran Church . . ."

At that point the twenty-dollar bill interrupts, "What's a church?"

observation

Bill-pay Giving Option

The quickest way to get up and running with electronic giving is to encourage your church members to use the bill-pay feature for their online banking. Those in the generation X and millennial groups are already doing this with their monthly expenses, and many baby boomers are embracing it as well. Adding the church as a recipient is easy for them.

Downloadable Pledge Card

Many churches have been successful in incorporating a way to pledge online. They use a downloadable pledge card for the members to fill out. While you can stop there and have them print it out and return it to the church, go the extra bit and enable a way for them to send it in electronically. Whatever route you go, make sure they get a prompt electronic receipt from your treasurer so that your donor knows their intentions have been received.

Donate Through the Church's Website

More and more churches are having success with members giving directly to their church by donating through the church website. This works the best with those who are giving about $100 to $200 dollars a month to your church. They can sign up to have their bank account debited each month for a set amount. This is the *set it and forget it* mentality. There are quite a few companies that offer this service to churches. Each has its own schedule of transaction fees, minimum or maximum amounts, and other limitations. Search out which one best suits the needs of your church.

Another benefit of setting up online giving is so your donors can go to the website and give a specific amount. This is most useful for special giving opportunities like supporting your church's Habitat for Humanity build.

The Evangelical Lutheran Church of America lists ten stewardship principles for its members to live by. One of them is *contribute regularly.* By setting up a monthly electronic giving program, you make it that much easier for your members to accomplish that.

If you are at a church that is hesitant to join online giving, you risk collecting fewer donations as the move to electronic banking and giving become more widespread. Electronic transactions are becoming more secure, increasing the trust your donors have when they contribute. Raise more money through consistent giving when your people sign up. Don't continue to be at the mercy of receiving contributions only when people show up to worship or remember to mail in a check.

However you decide to make electronic giving available to your church members, when presenting the options to your members, focus on the ease and convenience this type of giving offers. Churches have been suggesting weekly or monthly giving for decades, mostly through offering envelopes and, of course, offering baskets. Monthly giving has become the growing edge in secular fundraising. In that sector, a monthly-giving program is most effective by registering directly with the organization through its website.

How to Keep the Collection Basket Full

The downside of offering a way to give electronically is that when the collection basket comes by, there is nothing for people to put into it—they have already given! These donors are no longer participating in the offering *during* the worship service. A simple way to correct that is to provide a laminated card for people to place in the offering plate. This card says something like, "I gave electronically." It allows them to remain a part of the ritual of the collection and presentation of the financial offerings during the worship service. Their contribution is joined with the others and offered to God.

A tip we picked up from one church is to laminate the card so that it can be reused. The lamination makes them durable. Simply stock them in the pew racks each Sunday.

Mobile Giving

A final aspect of electronic giving that we want to cover includes mobile giving. Using card readers like you see at most checkout lines has arrived at church. One church uses the card-reader that connects directly to a cell phone or tablet for youth fundraising events. It is also a popular way to pay for extras that come up at church such as the ladies' luncheon or the seniors' outing to a concert.

Teach the Children and Youth to Give

Teaching the children and youth of your congregation to give is not really new. But what is new are the methods of teaching. Equipping our young to manage their money in a responsible manner is an important lifelong tool just like learning to read and to cook. Begin by examining your own relationship to money at a young age. Then assess how your church approaches this topic among your youngest members.

The following questions may be helpful for you to consider:

◆ What is your earliest memory of giving in the church? What is your child's?

Community Activities Interrupt Giving Cycle

One church in Atlanta experiences a significant decrease in its plate offerings four times a year. This is a church that heavily depends on the plate offerings, since few of its members subscribe to electronic monthly giving or mail in their contributions. The reason that these four Sundays are so consistently down in collections from the four weeks is because the church members can't get to their church on those days. You see, their church is on the route of four marathon races, and the roads and access to the church are shut off for the entire Sunday morning! Unfortunately, people don't make up for their missed Sunday; the church just loses revenue. Transitioning more members to electronic monthly giving would help to mitigate their losses.

 stories from the real world

◆ What are we teaching our children about giving or tithing? Anything at all?

◆ What kind of signals do we send our children about money? How do we spend on them as a church—do they get the worst meeting rooms and hand-me-down furniture while adults get the nicest rooms and new furnishings? Teach the youth that we value them.

◆ Do we give opportunities for youth and children to give each week? The opportunities can be in Sunday school, children's chapel, or the corporate worship service.

Many churches these days are successfully including their children and youth in the giving life of the congregation. Marketers are keenly aware that this young generation has more disposable income than any before it. Are you teaching your young people about giving back? Do you give them the opportunity to become active givers every week?

Include the Little Ones in Giving

There is a United Methodist church in Kentucky that has a children's offering every week. It is collected separately while the children and youth are in Sunday school. Each month, a different class—middle school through high school—counts the money and works with the treasurer to put it into an account. That class also gets to choose the recipient ministry by suggesting three ministries and voting among them within their own class.

Diversity of Giving

Innovations in church fundraising are not just about electronic giving. Do your pledge program materials reflect the language spoken by all of your members? You might consider translating your materials into Spanish or Korean if that is a language for a significant number of your members. The concept of a steward—or *mayordomo*—is slightly different in the Latin American culture, and doesn't necessarily include financial giving. Take care to communicate to your members in a way that takes their culture and traditions into account. Do all you can to help each member of your congregation learn the concepts of Christian stewardship.

To Recap

◆ The way money is used for transactions is rapidly changing. Our culture is moving away from writing checks and using cash to contribute to their church.

◆ Electronic giving offers a safe, convenient, and consistent way for giving money to your church.

◆ Be sure to teach the children and youth in your congregation what it means to manage their resources—include sharing both individually and as a church.

◆ Using a broader definition of stewardship than just financial giving will equip your members in a more deeply spiritual way than just talking about financial giving.

Chapter Twelve

Your Annual Pledge Drive May Be in October, But Stewardship Is All Year

IN THIS CHAPTER

◆ Develop a strategy for highlighting areas of stewardship

◆ Talk about money when you aren't asking for it—Jesus did!

◆ The T3 Myth: Time ≠ Talent ≠ Treasure

◆ Plan to Thank

You have probably heard the complaint, "All we hear about in church is money." While that is not likely the case, it is a common misconception. That is where the culture of your church needs to shift from a model that only talks about money and fundraising in the fall, to a community that talks about being stewards of God's gifts to them all year long.

To do this, you must first give the word "stewardship" a rebranding. For decades, we in the church have tarnished its meaning. This chapter will define what it means to be a steward of God's gifts, and give you suggestions on how to talk about being a good steward of these gifts in every season. Examine the fallacies of the time, talent, and treasure trio, and incorporate best practices for engaging your congregation in meaningful ways throughout the year. *Stewardship* will no longer be a dirty word, and church attendance during your fall pledge drive won't be low anymore.

In the first chapter of Genesis, after God created humankind in God's image, humans were given dominion over every living thing that lives and moves upon the earth. We were given custody, if you will, of all that God created. Custody can be defined as the protective care or guardianship of someone or something. We see in Psalm 24 that it still belongs to God when we read, "The earth is the Lord's and all that is in it." We are the caretakers or stewards for what belongs to God. To help your church members become good stewards, offer learning opportunities for them to embrace all aspects of stewardship. This can be accomplished by adding areas of focus to the church calendar.

The Goal of Stewardship

The ultimate goal of stewardship as a way of life is to develop disciples and to support them as they grow. This takes time and happens over a period of months and years. That's why we encourage talking about how to manage the gifts entrusted to you all year long. As a ministry leader, you should consider this an intentional effort to strengthen and support your members in their understanding of their roles as God's stewards.

principle

We suggest dividing up the calendar year and assigning themes of stewardship to each segment. You can have a new theme each month or each quarter. During this time, it is key to offer educational opportunities as well as activities for your members. Allowing them both intellectual and physical ways to interact with the concepts you present will offer a greater chance of their grasping the concepts. Design a strategy for the whole year—you can always add to it or modify it as you go. But if you start with a full stewardship plan, you can be sure the important areas are covered.

If your congregation is new to this idea of year-round stewardship, we suggest you add only two or three new activities the first year. It is better to do those few things well than to plan twelve or twenty-four activities that are marginally well executed. As you plan, first consider where you can include events or educational offerings you already are doing. You might find that a slightly higher emphasis on or adding a few details to current activities will round out the theme for the month. Perhaps adding a component in your worship service or Wednesday night programming will sufficiently elevate a theme.

Using themed topics enables your church to approach stewardship in a more holistic way. There are several good models for how to divide up the year. The Evangelical Lutheran Church in America uses themes of earth keeping, growth, giftedness, finances, lifestyle, and planning. The Presbyterian Foundation year-round design says to offer a different mission or ministry interpretation and promotion along with stewardship education each month. The Episcopal Diocese of West Texas suggests having an aspect of creation, spiritual growth, ministry spotlight, financial health, and outreach allotted to each month.

A quick internet search will yield these and several other models for how to approach talking about stewardship all year long. Or you could simply look at what secular activities happen throughout the calendar and match them up with appropriate church topics. The table we've included shows another approach. The important thing is to get started doing something now, and maintain it. This effort at year-round stewardship should be consistent throughout the year. One single push will not get you where you want to go—cultivate disciples who understand that stewardship is a spiritual matter, not a financial one.

Talking about money—our relationship to it—all throughout the year, but not asking for it, will give your members the opportunity to examine their personal habits around money. Jesus did this often and we read about it in each of the Gospels. Jesus knew that one of the challenges of our humanity is that our relationship to what we have gets in the way of our relationship with our Creator.

Lectionary-based Churches

Most lectionary-based churches use the Revised Common Lectionary, or RCL. The RCL sets forth a three-year cycle in which specific scripture—both Old and New Testament—readings are assigned each Sunday. It is intended to offer churches a wide breadth of scripture readings that cover a large portion of the Bible, and helps to avoid the tendency to use only a handful of passages over and over.

Year-round Stewardship

Month	Theme	Activity
January	Giving statements from last year (the first year will likely only be financial)	Reflect on your giving history and make resolutions on how you want this year to go.
February	Self-examination: How have you lived your life? Is that how you want your legacy to be?	Planned giving activities—education on tools of planned giving, what it has helped your church achieve in the past, and appropriateness of naming the church in your estate plans
March	Personal finances	Examine your spending habits—is your money going where you think it is? Classes on personal finance.
April	Creation	Plant a garden, recycle/reduce/reuse education, alternative transportation to church Sunday.
May	Spiritual gifts	Spiritual Gifts workshop—discerning your gifts
June	Time	Be intentional about your relaxation with family and friends. Unplug from TV and electronics. Make time to meditate and pray.
July	Pastoral care	Highlight the ministry that makes casseroles for shut-ins.
August	Care of self	Have you had your yearly physical? Nutrition classes, yoga, or tai chi classes. Start a running group.
September	Back to school: stewardship of our children	Parenting classes, grandparenting classes, godparenting classes
October	Annual pledge drive	Preach stewardship, testimonials in church: "Why I give."
November	Giving thanks for God's blessings	Thanksgiving service, bring in items that symbolize what you are thankful for. Thank-you notes for pledges.
December	Giving to others	Sponsor specific ministry needs (both in the church and in your community) with an ornament tree, and encourage people to buy the gift listed on the ornament which directly supports the ministry.

Lectionary-based churches will encounter numerous Sundays that speak to our relationship to money and other areas of stewardship. If your church is not lectionary-based, we offer some scriptural references to use as the basis of your teaching and preaching. We have already mentioned many passages in this book, and have listed Gospel references in **Chapter Six.** Here are a few more to consider that are broader in scope and refer to giving of one's self and other matters of stewardship.

- Psalm 24: 1-10, God as giver

- Psalm 50:14, 23a/ Hebrews 12:28/ Colossians 3:15—Being thankful to God

- Matthew 6:21—Where your treasure is

- Mark 10:23-27—It is easier for a camel to enter the kingdom of heaven

- Luke 12:48—Responsibility of giving

- II Corinthians 8:3-7—Giving voluntarily

- Acts 2:1-11—The disciples receive the gifts of the Holy Spirit

- I Timothy 6: 17-19—Be rich in good works, generous, and ready to share

Take the opportunities the secular calendar presents and use them to your advantage. At tax time, you might teach on personal budgeting, and "rendering to Caesar what is Caesar's," with the goal to help people examine if they are, then, rendering to God what is God's—themselves. At Christmas time, when there is a lot of emphasis on spending, big-reduction sales, and cyber-Monday, remind people that the real gift at Christmas is God's Son.

Spending a lot of money on gifts is not the goal. Rather, it is preparing oneself to welcome the Christ-child into your heart and home. Encourage your members to spend differently—spend time with friends and loved ones, spend time in service to others, and reflect on how to receive gifts from others.

A common trap that leaders of the stewardship ministry fall into is elevating talent and time with treasure. Many committees feel that if each is on the pledge card, that people will generously give all three. That is not the case, however. By having blank lines for your members to fill out next to time, talent, and treasure, most will see this as an opportunity to select one, and then feel their responsibility is complete.

They will likely pick the first item (it is a common phenomenon in voting), and it appears to be the easiest to fulfill. The problem with having all three options on a pledge card is that churches need all three *in abundance* to do the work of God. The church needs volunteers who offer their time by folding, stuffing, and stamping. The church needs people who offer their talent of balancing the financial accounts and flower arranging, regardless of the time involved. And the church needs members who offer of their financial means to cover everything else that needs accomplishing in ministries. We recommend using multiple pledge cards during the year.

Make Giving Easy

When filling out a pledge card, people will pick what is easiest—both on their schedule and their wallets.

When you talk about each ministry from your year-round stewardship plan, highlight the volunteer opportunities that are appropriate to each. Then provide a way for people to sign up. When you talk about spiritual gifts and talents, give people a talent pledge card so they can identify their specific skills. And during your fall pledge drive, offer an estimate-of-giving card that only asks for money.

The exception to this is during new-member classes. Just as you would instruct new members on the various ministry opportunities and how to use the childcare, include some education on the giving life of your congregation. Make the pledge cards a part of their new-member packet and give them examples of how others who are members reply.

At the same time, you are designing the activities for your members to interact with the themes of stewardship, include in a section of the plan to thank them throughout the year. Donors/stewards should be thanked for their time and talent as well as for their financial contributions. Showing your gratitude is, frankly, good stewardship of your volunteers and donors, and should be shown in a variety of ways. Of course, a handwritten thank-you note (from the stewardship chair person or committee member) should be sent to each member who returns a pledge card.

> ### Paul's Gratefulness
>
> *I give thanks to my God always for you because of the grace of God that has been given you.*
>
> —From Paul's letter to the people of Corinth
>
> **principle**

If you produce a monthly or twice-monthly newsletter, be sure to thank those who have participated by name. The same names can also be listed on your website.

An appropriate way to show your appreciation to those who volunteer their time and skills is to verbally thank them, perhaps during the announcement portion of your worship service. And for donors/stewards who go above and beyond, a reception in their honor can be held. By using a combination of these methods, your volunteers will be willing to share their time and talents the next time they are asked.

After you've invested twelve months on matters of stewardship, how do you know if it is having any effect? Can you point to signs that your members see stewardship as discipleship? Have you seen evidence of generosity in the congregation? This can be in the form of new pledges or an increase in individual pledge amounts. Establish some measurable outcomes and review them after each pledge drive. The results will help you know what you are doing right and what areas could use some improvement next year.

To Recap

- ◆ Your strategy for year-round stewardship should offer activities for people to grow spiritually in their understanding of holistic stewardship.

- ◆ Follow Jesus' model of talking about money but not asking for it every time.

- ◆ Ideally, people give of their time *and* their skills or talents, *and* from their financial resources.

- ◆ Show appreciation to those who give to your church, whether they volunteer their time, share their skills, or offer their financial resources.

Conclusion

I n this book, we have covered fundamentals of successful fundraising in churches and faith-based organizations. We have explored the three secrets to successful fundraising, and how to approach increasing giving by demonstrating the impact your church has on its members and the communities it serves. The bottom line is that you as a leader in your church are charged with making sure its ministries are funded and that your members understand the impact your church has on increasing sharing God's love through the ministries of your church.

In fact, just as there were twelve tribes of Israel and twelve disciples of Jesus, there are twelve things every church leader should know to be successful in making sure your ministries are funded:

- ◆ You need to make stewardship a priority in the life of your church.

- ◆ Your case for support must inspire your church members to give to your church ministries.

- ◆ Your leadership sets the tone that others in the congregation will take their cues from; set the right tone!

- ◆ Your plan must be well thought out and incorporate the natural rhythm of your church calendar.

- ◆ Everyone who walks through your door—and some who don't—can be asked to give.

- ◆ Remember to bring it back to this basic premise: Stewardship is a spiritual matter, not a financial one.

- ◆ Annual campaigns are essential and require careful planning.

- ◆ A good major gifts strategy is needed from time to time for special projects.

- ◆ Plan now for your next capital campaign—the actions you take today will impact your future ask.

- ◆ A consistent message that your church is an appropriate place to include in your estate plan is essential for the future of your church.

- ◆ Digital innovations must be integrated into your stewardship strategy.

- ◆ Talking about the importance of taking good care of all of God's gifts should take place all year.

Twelve things are a lot to include when you want to increase giving at your church, but implemented over several months, it should result in significantly more resources to carry out the work of God in your church. If you follow these practices, you will be successful in raising more funds for your church's mission.

Good luck and may God bless you!

Addendum A

Sample Narrative Budget Worksheet

Grace Church

The 2018 Proposed Church Budget totals $xxx,xxx, to be used as budgeted in the following areas of mission and ministry for the building up of God's Kingdom in our midst.

Worship

Sermon preparation, bulletin preparation, worship planning, Sunday morning worship, special services, scheduling lay liturgical leaders.

Compensation	
Operations/Overhead	
Direct Program Cost	
TOTAL	

Christian Formation/Education

Christian formation, baptism/confirmation/marriage preparation, VBS, Safe Church.

Compensation	
Operations/Overhead	
Direct Program Cost	
TOTAL	

Outreach

Parish events, ecumenical relationships, service to diocesan committees/programs, publicity for special events, community bulletin board, building usage, food and clothing ministry.

Compensation	
Operations/Overhead	
Direct Program Cost	
TOTAL	

Pastoral Care

Hospital and home visits/communion, individual/crises/grief response pastoral counseling.

Compensation	
Operations/Overhead	
Direct Program Cost	
TOTAL	

Parish Life/Fellowship

Parish suppers, coffee hour, postcards/e-mails/other special notes.

Compensation	
Operations/Overhead	
Direct Program Cost	
TOTAL	

Communications

Dealing with the website, newsletters, printing, electronic media, writers & editors, including notifying media of special services and reporting of church events, publicity for special events.

Compensation	
Operations/Overhead	
Direct Program Cost	
TOTAL	

Addendum B

Sample Narrative Budget

[Starts on the next page.]

Welcome Along Our Journey...

St. Nicholas Episcopal Church is a place where the Holy Spirit is alive and well, working through and among us to accomplish God's incredible vision. Our ministries are thriving and our community has never been better.

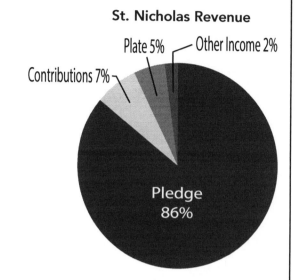

St. Nicholas Revenue

Plate 5%   Other Income 2%

Contributions 7%

Pledge 86%

In 2017, here is how St. Nicholas put your contributions to work!

Pastoral Care

Taking care of those in need is one of our most important activities. From taking Holy Communion to our shut--ins to providing prayer support and counseling to those who are ill or in crisis, our ongoing care exemplifies our Christian community. Lay ministers and clergy provide pastoral care in the following ways:

Home Visitation • Hospital Visits • Funeral Services • Bereavement Counseling • Baptisms • Premarital Counseling • Shut-in Visits • Prayer Blankets

Outreach

As an expression of our faith, we have chosen to contribute 18% of operating revenues to outreach. We believe that Christ's face can be seen any time we humble ourselves enough to put the needs of anyone else above our own. The projects, which have a parish and community, and world--wide impact, include:

FOCUS • Chattahoochee Valley Episcopal Ministries • Relay for Life • Episcopal Relief & Development • Compassion International • Diocesan Pledge

Communications

Good communications are critically important to the life of our congregation and currently accounts for 15% of our total operating expenses. As the generational make-up of our congregation continues to become more diverse, it is important to communicate in a variety of ways. This includes:

Website • Newsletter • Bulletins • Facebook/Twitter • Publicity/Advertising

Worship

The most significant part of our ministry funding goes toward worship. Our expressions of worship are as diverse as our members with a variety of songs of praise and worship styles. Included in this area are the following ministries and activities:

Acolytes • Altar Guild • Lay Eucharistic Ministers • Readers • Choir • Blessing of the Animals • Weddings • Funerals • Baptisms • Nursery Workers • Bulletins • Ushers • Greeters • Bluegrass Mass • Flower Guild • Worship at Blue Springs • Pulpit Swap with Christian Valley Church

Christian Education

Spiritual formation may come in many ways. The most obvious is through learning, and St. Nicholas has a rich history of valuing education. We are committed to offering all our people – adults, children and youth – a variety of opportunities to learn about the Christian faith.

SNICK (St. Nicholas Kids) • Youth Group • Diocesan Youth Events • Lenten Series • Sunday School • Adult Forum • Bible Study

Parish Life

Whether it's an after--church potluck lunch or a swinging seasonal party, St. Nicholas takes getting together to enjoy each other seriously. Jesus knew the importance of table fellowship, and as his followers, we continue the tradition of gathering and sharing a bit of ourselves with each other. Some of these activities are:

Lobsterfest • Easter Reception/Egg Hunt • Trunk or Treat • Thanksgiving Potluck • Christmas Tea • Mardi Gras • Annual Meeting Luncheon • Epiphany Party

The operating budget income for 2017 totals $226,500. The expenses, including what is expected through the rest of the year, are $224,995. The chart to the right is intended to convey a real picture of what we are doing through the generosity of our members and friends. In this graphic and narrative form, we demonstrate the areas of ministry in which we are currently actively involved.

St. Nicholas Expenses

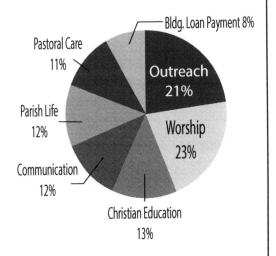

Index

Did you know that CharityChannel Press is the fastest growing publisher of books for busy nonprofit professionals? Here are some of our most popular titles.

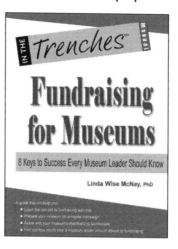

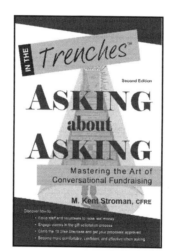

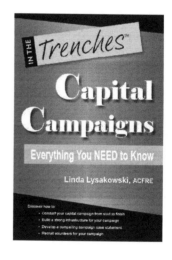

CharityChannel.com/bookstore

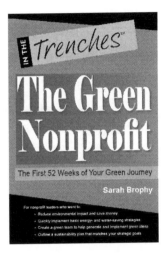

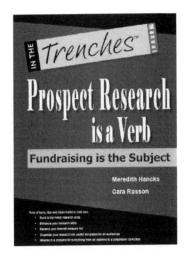

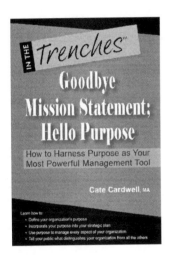

CharityChannel.com/bookstore

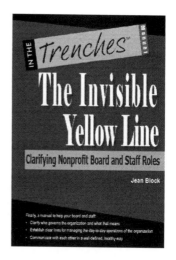

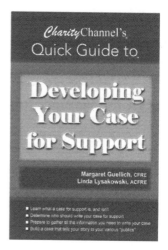

CharityChannel.com/bookstore

And more!

Made in the USA
Middletown, DE
05 May 2017